Scholarship and Technology
in the
Humanities

Scholarship and Technology in the Humanities

Proceedings of a Conference held at Elvetham Hall, Hampshire, UK, 9th-12th May 1990

Edited by May Katzen

British Library Research

BOWKER
SAUR ●

London • Melbourne • Munich • New York

British Library Cataloguing in Publication Data

A catalogue record for this book is available from the British Library

AZ105
536
1991

Bowker-Saur is part of the Professional Division of Reed International Books, 60 Grosvenor Street, London W1X 9DA

Cover design by John Cole
Printed on acid-free paper
Printed and bound in Great Britain by
Antony Rowe, Chippenham, Wilts.

Preface

This volume of papers derives from an international conference on Scholarship and Technology in the Humanities, held in May 1990, at Elvetham Hall, Hampshire. The conference aimed to bring together a group of participants representing scholars, librarians, computer experts, publishers, and funding agencies from the United Kingdom, Continental Europe, and the United States, to explore the implications of the rapidly increasing and irreversible penetration of technology into all phases of scholarly communication in the humanities over the past two decades.

The idea of such a conference initially arose from the activities of the Office for Humanities Communication, a centre established in 1982 by the British Library to act as national focus for all aspects of information and communication in the humanities, particularly in relation to the impact of the use of computers on research and teaching. Soundings taken in the UK and abroad indicated that there was widespread enthusiasm for the idea, and wholehearted agreement that the time had come to consider how, and to what extent, the prevalence of electronic information media and systems had influenced the direction, the content, and the methods of research in the humanities disciplines, and what steps should be taken to ensure that the humanities could benefit from the burgeoning proliferation of new technologies in academic institutions, in libraries, and in publishing.

Accordingly, an Organizing Committee was set up in 1989, under the chairmanship of Mr J.M. Smethurst, Director General of the British Library, Humanities and Social Sciences. It consisted of two sections, which represented a range of appropriate institutions and individuals concerned with humanities research in Europe (including the UK) and the United States respectively. The two sub-committees collaborated closely in planning the programme of the conference and selecting the participants. The aim was to provide a forum for a wide-ranging, lively discussion among a selection of key actors involved in creating and sustaining scholarship in the humanities, regarding the main issues and the implications of the conduct of research and education in an environment increasingly shaped and mediated by technology; and, in the light of the deliberations of the conference, to come to conclusions which might point the way for future, necessary action in this field. The intention was to avoid the minutiae of particular technological tools, but rather to focus and reflect upon the general import for scholars and scholarship of recent and possible future changes in information and communication in the humanities.

The three day conference was sponsored by the Andrew W. Mellon Foundation, the British Library, the British Academy, the American Council of Learned Societies, the Council on Library Resources, the Research Libraries Group and Apple Computer Ltd. These bodies together generously provided the necessary funding for the meeting.

From the outset, it was intended that the conference should be the springboard for a publication on the theme of Scholarship and Technology in the Humanities. The high level and wide-ranging scope of the pre-circulated commissioned papers, and the lively debates and controversies that ensued at Elvetham Hall, reinforced this decision, as did the deep interest both before and after the conference among all the constituencies concerned with the humanities—academics, university administrators, librarians, archivists, learned societies, publishers, and funding agencies—in Europe and the United States. This volume consists of a selection of some of the papers prepared for the conference, revised in the light of the discussions, introduced by an overview of some of the main themes that emerged, and concluding with the recommendations made by the delegates regarding matters which, in their opinion, required urgent action.

May Katzen

Contents

Appendices

Introduction

May Katzen

Office for Humanities Communication

Over the past ten or fifteen years, there has been an escalating interest on the part of humanities scholars in the continually widening possibilities of using computers in their work. Witness the ever-growing numbers of new learned societies, newsletters, journals and books, as well as conferences, devoted to every conceivable aspect of computing in the humanities. Concomitantly, there has been a veritable explosion of increasingly user friendly, affordable and relevant computer based tools and a growing volume of resources in machine-readable form in a variety of media capable of serving the needs of research and teaching in the humanities. To a greater or lesser extent, the computer is present at every step in the communication chain. It is becoming ever more likely that the humanist will not only use a wordprocessor instead of a typewriter, but will retrieve reference information electronically from computer based catalogues, indexes and abstracts, analyze research material converted to machine-readable form, submit monographs and articles to publishers on disc, communicate with colleagues and exchange data on wide and local area networks, read books and journals which have been created, edited and composed by computer assisted methods, and teach students with the aid of computers.

It is clear that the application of electronic information technologies to scholarly communication activities in the humanities is no mere flash in the pan, nor a passing fashionable fad, nor the exclusive province of a small band of enthusiastic (or over-enthusiastic) devotees. The use of computerized tools is becoming ever more deeply entrenched into all the phases of the creation, collection, storage, and dissemination of humanities scholarship. Rightly employed, these tools have proved so efficacious, both in enabling traditional scholarly activities to be undertaken more quickly and thoroughly than before, as well as in enabling new techniques to be developed, that they are likely to become an increasingly pervasive, permanent part of the furniture of scholarship. This situation poses a number of interesting questions in relation to the present and possible future impact of electronic technologies on scholarly practices, on the content and direction of research, on the modes of higher education in humanities disciplines, and on the infrastructure of scholarly communication.

In seeking to assess the impact of technology on the humanities, one may consider its effects on the interdependent series of activities that constitutes the research communication chain, which extends from the scholar *qua* author, through the publisher and bookseller to the library and thence to the ultimate user of scholarship, the reader, whether researcher or student.

As Anthony Kenny's paper demonstrates (see below pp. 1–10) the communication system, as it has come to operate in recent years (largely as the result of the dominance of the competitive ethos in academic life, in conjunction with the retrenchment of academic salaries, student grants and library budgets) is skewed towards benefiting the producers of research—authors and publishers—while putting increasing burdens of cost and information overload on the consumers of research, libraries and readers.

On the whole, the application of technology to communication activities has tended to mirror, or to complement, the traditional processes of the creation, distribution, storage and use of scholarship, rather than to transform them. Broadly speaking, the result has been to reinforce, rather than to mitigate these underlying strains in the system.

The provision of technological aids has provided undoubted opportunities and advantages, but at the same time can create problems. The use of computer based facilities provides the advantages of speed, accuracy and comprehensiveness to the location and analysis of research materials. These advantages have made libraries and researchers more efficient, while authors and publishers have benefited from wordprocessing and from computer aided editing and composition. But technology can also have its down side. Scholars may be tempted to concentrate on software development rather than on scholarship, highly ingenious systems may be created which are too expensive or complicated for general use; or research may be polarized between projects which are easily amenable to computerization, undertaken by the computer literate, while those who loathe computers and statistics may perhaps be driven to concentrate on increasingly abstract, intuitive work. There is also a danger that a dichotomy may develop between large, expensive, well-funded computer based research, undertaken by research groups which combine a variety of disciplinary and computer expertise, and more traditional projects undertaken by individuals who may find it difficult to compete successfully for the funding they require.

Similar strains and conflicting demands are also affecting libraries, particularly national libraries. They may be forced to choose between the acquisition of increasingly expensive new books and journals, the maintenance and preservation of their existing traditional holdings of manuscripts and printed material, and building up their stocks of electronically based resources, between purchasing new machines and software, keeping or hiring new skilled staff, and undertaking the expensive, time consuming, though ultimately worthwhile conversion of manual methods and instruments of bibliographic control to automated procedures and systems.

Above all, the switch from traditional to technologically based methods of creating, retrieving, organizing, and analyzing information not only entails the additional costs of hardware and software, but always involves the looming threat of technological obsolescence—the inevitable consequence of rapid technological development and change. Thus, for example, the very real possibility exists that machine-readable resource materials, on which a great deal of time, effort and money may have been spent, may become impossible to use in a relatively short time because the software and hardware with which they are associated will be superseded by newer, incompatible technologies. International efforts are under way (via the Text Encoding Initiative) to provide encoding standards for digitized text and data, which, if they become widely followed, will enhance the portability of electronically based resources created in the future, though widespread retrospective encoding may be difficult and expensive to achieve. In any case, the continuing proper maintenance of material in a variety of electronic media and formats, held in specialized archives, computer centres, libraries and even in departments is, *ipso facto*, time-consuming and costly, and underscores the economic consequences of the increasing dependence on technology, especially during an era of financial retrenchment. This is only one instance, among a range of others, which imposes the need for organized effort and rationalization, and, above all, for collaboration and collective

decision making at all levels—institutional, national and international—
to try to ensure the continued availability of and access to electronic, as
well as traditional resources for scholarship, research and teaching in the
humanities.

Keynote Address

Technology and Humanities Research

Anthony Kenny
The British Academy

We are all familiar with the concept of the food chain. In a similar sense there is a research chain: or perhaps one should say, more accurately, a research communication chain. The chain of research communication links together researcher, author, publisher, bookseller, librarian, reviewer, and reader. In the humanities one can say, with a slight exaggeration, that the chain of research communication is a closed one. Producers and consumers are the same community: the standard reader of academic publications is a researcher, and it is in reading, above all, that research in the arts consists. The different members of the communication chain have a common interest in the continued operation of the chain; but their interests can also diverge.

In the present lecture I want to identify the principal ways in which the development of technology has had an impact on the different points of the chain of research communication, from researcher through writer, through publisher, through bookseller, through librarian, through reviewer, to reader. I want in this way to put us into a position to evaluate the effect which the new technology has had on the whole academic cycle in the humanities.

If we are to judge whether the research communication industry is serving its purpose well, we have to decide on what the goal of research is, and what is the point of communicating the results of research. Here there may well be different perceptions on the part of those who carry out research and those who fund it. Many universities, particularly in the US where they like to be explicit about such things, will have in their charters some such phrase as that they exist for the education of the citizens, the pursuit of knowledge, and the welfare of mankind.

Academic researchers like to think that by discovering new scientific truth, or refining the historical record, or making the art and literature of the past accessible to the present, they are *eo ipso* conferring a benefit on the human race (whether or not their results are 'exploitable' in any crude sense). Those who provide funds for research, whether private or public, are more likely to have in mind the possibility that research will increase the economic potential of the nation. Scholars tend to think of themselves as members of an international community, 'The Republic of Learning'; funders of research tend to think of the citizens of other countries as 'Our Competitors'.

Funders of research are unlikely to be impressed by the ideal of a republic of scholars who pursue scholarship for scholarship's sake. They are likely to be tempted to axe funding for non-exploitable research, and to depress academic salaries in areas which do not contribute to the competitive advancement of the national economy. Funding bodies also tend to have their priorities and their procedures dominated by the model of the sciences which are productive of concrete economic benefits.

There are, however, important differences between research in the sciences and in the humanities. In the sciences, the collaborative research project is the norm. In the arts, while excellent work has been done in recent years by teams of scholars in collaboration, it remains true that most research is characteristically individualistic, and is likely to remain so. In some areas of the humanities the scope for using research assistants is minimal. If one's concern is not with amassing factual data, but with the interpretation and modification of concepts, or the critical response to a literary text, one cannot easily delegate any reading to an assistant. And this is so whether the assistant is human or electronic.

At the present time there are strains on the existing system of research and research communication, arising from two sources: namely, technological development and the prevailing ethos of competition. The effects of technology on research and research publishing in scientific subjects have long been obvious; but in the arts, too, technological developments now affect the researcher (whether he studies texts and uses concordances, or whether he amasses and analyzes quantitative data), the writer (who is more and more likely to compose on a wordprocessor), the publisher (who has at his disposal new methods of book production, and new media of publication), the librarian (who will use computers for cataloguing and circulation control), the reader (who has access now to facsimile, hypertext and other novel aids to study), and the bookseller (who will exploit the new technology in many ways which others present will know better than I do).

The competitive ethos, once thought foreign to academe, now affects the daily life of academics, through the emphasis placed by government, and subsequently, however reluctantly, by university authorities, upon assessment by performance indicators. The threat of competitive evaluation provides a spur to academics to publish if they are not to perish, so that an increased number of books is offered to publishers. At a time of trimming of library funding, the response of publishers to this pressure has been to publish more titles with shorter print runs and faster remaindering. Hence follow longer reading lists for students, and more problems for academics who wish to keep up with publications in their field. As more books are published in scholarly subjects, the marginal return to the scholar from reading them becomes less and less. The competitive ethos, in my view, presents a much more serious long term threat to traditional scholarship than any developments in technology. But it is technology, not competition, which is our present concern.

Where, in fact, are we to look for the major effects of technological developments in humanities research? The most spectacular is the creation of the whole new topic of research, the new discipline of computational linguistics. The most widely felt effect has been the perfecting of traditional tools of research, data collections, concordances (at first output in hard copy, now much more likely to be consulted on a PC), dictionaries, and corpora. But in spite of these benefits, it is surprisingly difficult to point, in specific areas, to solid, uncontroverted gains to scholarship which could not have been achieved without the new technology.

The effect of technological change on humanities research can be exaggerated. It is true that scholars in the humanities are becoming more computer-literate, and the development of the personal computer, and the availability of packages which simplify quantitative analysis, have gone some way to bridge the two cultures which were described by C.P. Snow. Even Jane Austen is now studied with the aid of the computer, with results which are of genuine and original literary interest. But the high hopes which some computer enthusiasts held out that the computer would revolutionize humanistic study have been proved, over and over again, to be unrealistic. Sometimes the initial claims made were much exaggerated: as the claim made in New Testament studies that the computer would for the first time reveal the true lineaments of the Bible that we had ignorantly worshipped. But even in areas where there was no hubris in the initial claims, the results delivered have often been disappointing. Let me give two examples which I owe to Manfred Thaller.

In France, Gian Piero Zarri has developed a system known as RESE-DA to allow Artificial Intelligence techniques to be applied to historical source material (concerning the Hundred Years' War). The project is well known in AI circles; but it seems to have left virtually no trace in the historical literature. This is because the system is so complicated that no historian could use it without explicit support from the AI project group.

Again, in 1981-87 the Volkswagenstiftung funded on a large scale the ARCOS project, a system which photographs a three-dimensional archaeological object, provides a drawing and converts it into data which lend themselves easily to methods like Cluster Analysis. The prototype was in the vanguard of technical development. Unfortunately the price of the prototype was so high that it was out of the financial reach of the archaeological community.

So far I have been considering the effect of technological developments upon researchers in the humanities. The effect on the humanist as writer is more obvious. The virtues of wordprocessors are familiar to all of us. So are the vices, such as the constant temptation to authors to reproduce stale material in a new context; misbehaviour to which, in the past, the labour of actual copying would have acted as a deterrent. The writer as typesetter, thanks to the possibilities of desktop publishing, can now have far more control of the appearance of his text in a published version than was possible in the past. On the other hand, he may be tempted to spend time as an amateur on the design of layout which would have been better spent on improving the text which embodies his professional expertise.

I turn now to consider the effects of technological change on the dissemination of research. Will electronic media supersede the printed word, online or in CD-ROM form? My secondhand impression is that in spite of recent developments in the scope of electronic publishing, scholars still like journals, because of peer review, academic recognition, and good archiving. Despite decreases in demand due to funding cuts, publishers still seem to find it profitable to publish volumes of journals sold on subscription.

Will publishers try to bypass libraries—as journal publishing began to bypass the bookseller in the sixties? What seems most likely to happen in the humanities at least is that electronic mail and electronic bulletin boards will be a complement rather than a replacement of the journal system. Though many business and legal publications are online, the market for scholarly ones is likely to remain too limited for that to be the commercially preferable form of publishing.

What of the effect of the new technology on libraries? In a conference sponsored by the British Library it would be presumptuous of me to say much. But there seem to me to be three main aspects of the use of computers in libraries, about each of which I would like to hear more from the experts present. The first is the use of computers to assist in the location of material: computerized catalogues and circulation control in the individual library, and networking between different libraries. The second is the use of computers to assist the consultation of material: possibilities of different forms of searching through catalogues, and the development of abstracting services making use of standardized fields. The third is the use of new technologies which assist in the preservation of material: the production of facsimiles and various forms of icon which cut down on the need to handle fragile items with inevitable deterioration.

What is the effect of technology on the academic in the role of reviewer, or reviewee? The pursuit of value for money by funding agencies may lead to the desire to quantify the output which results from the making of a grant. The amount published by academics is the most easily measurable feature of comparison between them. Therefore when academics, departments, or universities are placed in competition relative to each other there is pressure to publish. This leads to a lowering of standards: those who have nothing much to say that is original may feel forced to pretend to. The standard, as well as the quantity of what is published, can of course be measured: there are citation indices to reveal how often an article by a researcher is quoted by his peers.

Many academics are scornful of such bibliometry: the citation index, they say, is worthless as an indicator of quality. I do not agree, certainly with respect to the humanities where there are not the problems of multiple authorship which beset the use of scientific citation indices for evaluation purposes. It is true that in my own subject, philosophy, one scholar rarely quotes another except to expose the foolishness of his conclusions and the flimsiness of his arguments. None the less, even in philosophy, bibliometry is neither impossible nor ridiculous. When I look up the citation index and count how many times my colleagues have been quoted in the past quarter, I find that the ranking given by the index is roughly the same as the one I would give if I were asked to take part in a peer review of them. Not only living philosophers appear in a citation index, of course, and it can be fun finding out, for instance, whether Aristotle is coming up and Heidegger going down in fashion.

It is true that how many people read a philosopher depends on how popular his subject matter may be. But in the index, popular subjects and unpopular ones can cancel out. I have written both on the philosophy of mind, which is a popular topic, and on the Eudemian Ethics, one of the most obscure of Aristotelian texts. There are about a hundred times as many philosophers of mind as there are students of the Eudemian Ethics: I find that I am quoted by no more than one in a hundred philosophers of mind, but on the other hand I am quoted by every one of the handful of writers on the Eudemian Ethics. So the citations break even.

But bibliometry is reliable only in certain conditions. One is that disciplines are in a more or less steady state. If you have a declining discipline, decline will be accelerated. If you are a classicist and there are fewer classicists around to quote you, your own and your colleagues' performance indicators will go down, and your own department will be axed if the university takes performance indicators seriously. On the other hand if you write a mediocre article in a field which is initially empty but happens to become fashionable, it will be quoted out of all proportion to its worth.

Even when they are reliable, bibliometric methods of evaluation carry disadvantages. They increase the already exaggerated impetus to publish: to be sure, good works are quoted more than bad works, but if you do not publish anything you will not be quoted at all. Overall, the emphasis on the easily quantifiable is likely to skew the effort of university staff. The quality of teaching is hard to judge and quantify, so a scholar who wishes to help a university achieve good ratings will throw the major effort into getting things published.

The time has come to ask what the forces we see in operation do to the person who stands at the end of the research chain: the reader. To answer this question let us follow for a moment the passion for quantification, and ask how many readers the typical academic research paper can expect to have. Estimates of the number of readers of scientific articles vary widely. Within the covers of a single, well-respected collection of professional studies[1] we find estimates of the number of readings per article ranging from 'a dozen' to 690 (Meadows, 1979i,ii).

Let us try to make an independent assessment of the likely number of readers of an article in a humanities subject. Let us assume—perhaps charitably—that the typical academic works a six-day week, ten hours a day, forty six weeks a year; that makes a working year of 2,760 hours. Let us make the assumption that thirty per cent of this working time is spent on research, the rest being devoted to teaching and administration. That gives 828 hours. Suppose we say our scholar spends half his research time reading and half his research time writing; and of his reading time, roughly one half reading books, and one half reading articles. That gives him just over two hundred hours article-reading time a year; and let us suppose each article takes one hour and no more to read. This means each academic will read about two hundred articles a year.

I want to consider the implications of these figures for my own subject, philosophy. In England and the US there are approximately 8,400 working philosophers. In English there are approximately 12,800 philosophy articles published each year. So the average philosopher writes one and a half articles a year; that seems a plausible, and not discreditable result.

But who reads the articles? Most such articles would be comprehensible only to professional philosophers; so the class of readers and the class of writers is probably coextensive. On the assumptions above, the mean number of times an article is read is (8,400 x 200)/12,800; that is to say, one hundred and thirty one times. Surely no one would publish a book with a print run as short as this: does it make sense to operate a system of publishing articles whose real readership is so small?

If this figure is even approximately right, there seems to be a question over the whole research communication chain. And of course it is very unrealistic to assume that each article has an equal chance of being read: we know that there are a few articles which everyone will read, and many articles which must never be read at all, other than by their writers and referees. One is bound to conclude that the research chain is heavily overloaded. The greater the pressure to publish, and therefore the more time the scholar spends writing rather than reading, the less chance there

---

1. I am indebted for this reference to Dr. M. Katzen.

is of each article being read. If prolonged, the effect of recent developments may be to bring the category of reader closer and closer to zero.

Let me conclude by summing up what I see as the dangers which technological developments present for scholarship. I can identify six, which I will call: redundancy of people, redundancy of effort, diversion of effort, diversion of funding, distortion of research and transfer of population.

1. Redundancy of people

Alexander Cruden spent the best years of his life preparing his concordance to the Bible. There is no longer any need for dedicated Crudens to make concordances. Classical scholars among us will all, as students, have stood in awe of our seniors who, given a rare Greek word, could pluck out of their memories the ten contexts in different classical authors in which it was used. Nowadays any student can discover the information in moments with the aid of IBYCUS. As Professor Connor says (see below p.60) it is no longer possible to found a reputation for scholarship on being good at spotting allusions. This problem is the humanistic analogue of the problem of the stoker on the electric train. It is not a serious one for the discipline, nor even in human terms does it compare with the undesirable side-effects of technological innovations in practical life and scientific research. Editors of classical texts may lament the wide availability of xerox, microform, and facsimile, because it takes away much of the justification of that most agreeable of academic pursuits, the *Biblioteksreise*. But luckily most manuscripts have enough ambiguous smudges to enable the pilgrimage to be justified after the microfilm has been read.

2. Redundancy of effort

Scholars who are good at knowing where to look for the sources of their subject matter may not be good at knowing where to look for suitable software. The replacement of mainframe use by desktop computing in recent years means that scholars working alone do not have as much contact with computer-learned people as they used to do. This means they are less in touch with software developments. Hence, if they become interested in designing their own software, scholars may spend their time reinventing last year's wheel.

3. Diversion of effort

Even if the software designed is genuinely original and useful, there is a danger that scholars become hooked on the production of software. There is a temptation that though you are drawing your salary as a historian or as a literary critic you spend most of your working time as a programmer.

4. Diversion of funding

Because there is pressure on departments in humanistic subjects to appear up-to-date and efficient, it is much easier to persuade funding bodies to give money for computers and software than to buy manuscripts, rare books, or second and third copies of frequently used library texts. After a few years a department may be left with serious gaps in its library and a load of superannuated computing equipment.

5. Distortion of research

There is a danger that projects may be undertaken not because they are likely to lead to academically interesting results, but simply because they are susceptible to computerization. In the words of Manfred Thaller 'we must adapt the software to the scholarship, not the scholarship to the software' (M. Thaller, 1990, personal communication). The danger here is not so much the effect of technology, as the effect of a technological ethos. Scholars feel the need to show they have used the latest technology, even if electronic methods are not the appropriate ones.

6. Transfer of population

Professor Connor, in his fascinating paper on computers in classical studies, claims that computers came just at the wrong time, at a time when scholars' interests were moving from textual studies to theory, women's studies and the like. He says:

> Computer technology became available precisely at the wrong moment in the profession's development. The era of traditional lexical and textual studies had largely passed... The energy of North American classicists, by and large, has concentrated on interpretive questions and on the writing of essays and monographs of social themes, cultural history and literary criticism... The questions posed by Feminist, Marxist, Structuralist and Post-Structuralist criticism have not lent themselves to computer-based responses.

Is this just a malign coincidence? One may well speculate on possible causes for the phenomenon. One does not need to draw exaggerated conclusions from the differences between the left and right hand sides of the brain in order to accept that humanists and scientists may be different kinds of people. Those whose gifts and tastes lie in a certain direction— people who do not have a head for mathematics—may well have been influenced by this in an early career choice. To their dismay they see quantification invading their own subject: they might as well have become physicists or engineers if English literature, Greek history and even New Testament theology now offer no escape from those wretched numbers. So now the more abstract, intuitive, and ideological branches of the humanities become more attractive. The number of practitioners in these areas grows—largely, no doubt, through the genuine fascination of their subjects, but swollen perhaps with an influx of refugees from the relentless advance of technological rigour. There are still, thank God, a few areas where one can work without either having to use computers or feeling guilty because one does not.

If this is a correct analysis of the situation, the consequences for our disciplines may be far-reaching in unexpected ways which are only just beginning to be noticed.

Reference

Meadows, A.J. (1979) Editor. **The Scientific Journal,** (i) p.61; (ii) p.48. London: Aslib.

Recent Trends in Different Disciplines

Literary Theory, Telecommunications, and the Making of History

J. Hillis Miller

University of California at Irvine

This essay begins with a brief description of the development of literary study in the United States since the 1950s.[2] It then relates those developments to technological innovations in computers and telecommunications during the same period. The problematic word here is 'relates'. The relation in question is multiple, non-linear, non-causal, non-dialectical, and heavily overdetermined. It does not fit most traditional paradigms for defining 'relationship'. Moreover, these two developments can only arbitrarily be separated from concomitant global changes in the social, political, industrial, economic, media, and institutional domains making up an immense moving web or network of simultaneous transformations. But 'web' or 'network' are inadequate linear metaphors for the strange topology, a non-spatial space constituted by sign to sign relations rather than by object to object relations. 'Signs' here includes alphabetic, iconic, visual, and auditory forms: words, pictures, and music interwoven in what is called interactive multimedia, 'interactive' because we can change it as it changes us. One use of the new technologies is to map

---

2. This description is drawn from an essay of mine on the development since the nineteenth century of literary studies in the United States. That essay was prepared for a conference in Beijing sponsored jointly by the Chinese Academy and Social Sciences and the American Academy of Arts and Sciences. The full essay will appear in *Divided Knowledge: Across Disciplines, Across Cultures* (1991), edited by D. Easton and C.S. Schelling. Newbury Park, CA: Sage Publications (in cooperation with the American Academy of Arts and Sciences).

in more adequate ways this new sign-space we all inhabit and that inhabits us. Such a brief paper can of necessity give only the tips of many icebergs. In an ideal 'hypertext' version of this essay each sentence would be a 'button' leading to an indefinitely large database expanding and specifying what that sentence says. Before long it will be possible to provide on disc such a version of an essay like this one. My topic is the implications of this fact for research, teaching, and writing about literature.

The most recent phase in the development of literary study in the United States has been the gradual importation and domestication of continental literary theories beginning in the '50s. This importation occurred at the same time as the myth criticism of a Canadian scholar, Northrop Frye, was exerting a strong influence in the United States. The wide appeal in the late 1950s of Frye's all-inclusive systematic typology of literature in his *Anatomy of Criticism* (1957) was evidence that teachers and students of literature were beginning to feel a need for an explicit theory of literature, a need not satisfied by the New Criticism.

By the mid-1960s, partly as a concomitant of political events like the Vietnam War, student activism, women's liberation, and the Civil Rights movement, conventional approaches to literary studies seemed increasingly inappropriate. Those who deplore the gradual triumph of the new theoretical approaches should remember that they were a response to a widely-felt sense of the detachment of traditional literary studies from social or personal usefulness. Theoretical work imported from the continent responded to that need for 'relevance'. First existentialism and phenomenology began to be assimilated as the basis of a new kind of criticism, and then in the '60s structuralism, Lacanian psychoanalysis, newer kinds of Marxist criticism, and Derridian deconstruction were brought in.

It is convenient to date the start of the second, more radical, wave of this primarily French invasion in 1966, the date of a structuralist symposium held at Johns Hopkins University and sponsored by the Ford Foundation. Papers from this symposium were published in *The Languages of Criticism and the Sciences of Man* (Macksey and Donato, 1970). This symposium was one of the earliest and most influential of that multitude of international conferences on literary theory that have now become commonplace almost everywhere in the world. The Hopkins symposium brought Jacques Lacan and Jacques Derrida to their first public appearances in the United States, along with representatives of a slightly older generation of phenomenological critics like Georges Poulet, and Marxist critics like Lucien Goldmann and the classicist Jean-Paul Vernant. American literary study since then has been increasingly dominated by these imported theories and by the assumption of a need to base literary study on explicitly theoretical reflection.

The present situation, in the study of literature in the United States, is, as I have elsewhere argued (Miller, 1987), characterized by the almost universal triumph of theory. This is true in spite of the continued active presence of what Paul de Man called 'the resistance to theory' (de Man, 1986).

I mean by the triumph of theory what is evident on every side, not only the development of a large number of powerful competing theoretical discourses, each with its somewhat barbarous code name—hermeneutic, phenomenological, Lacanian, feminist, reader response, Marxist, Foucaultian, structuralist, semiotic, deconstructionist, new historicist, cultural critical, and so on—but the accompanying immense proliferation of courses, curricula, books, textbooks, dissertations, essays, lectures, new journals, symposia, study groups, centres and institutes all overtly concerned with theory or with what is called 'cultural studies'. These taken together form a 'hidden university' crossing departmental, disciplinary, and institutional boundaries. Much of the frontier work in literary studies is taking place today in this hidden university. This is not the place to try to characterize each of the kinds of literary theory I have named. It takes Vincent Leitch a big book of over four hundred pages to sketch out the main modes and their presuppositions (Leitch, 1988). What needs to be stressed here is the large number of competing theories and their incoherence. They cannot be synthesized into some single grand all-inclusive theory of literature.

The victory of theory has transformed the field of literary study from what it was when I entered it forty years ago. In those happy days, we mostly studied primary works in the context of literary history, with some overt attention in our teaching to the basic presuppositions of the so-called New Criticism: the primacy of metaphor, the universality of the principle of organic unity, and so on. Now it is necessary to be acquainted with a large number of incompatible theories, each claiming our allegiance.

The present-day triumph of theory is no doubt overdetermined. It has many and incompatible 'causes', or, it would be better to say, 'associated factors', to try to avoid begging the question by slipping in the word 'causes'. The conflict of diverse assumptions among the different theories is one such factor, since their obvious incoherence forces theoretical reflection. If everyone shares the same assumptions, they can be taken for granted. Explicit theory does not appear to be necessary. Among other factors are demographic changes that are making the United States more and more a multilingual country, so that it makes less sense to base literary study exclusively on canonical works in English literature; the rise of the United States as a major world power accompanied by a decline in the power of England, another factor reducing the importance of literature written in England: it makes less sense now to have literary studies in American colleges and universities centred in 'Departments of English', if that means primarily literature written in England;[3] the women's movement, which has had and is having enormous effects on American culture; technological changes like the jetplane, which can bring scholars and critics from all over the world together for a conference, computers, tape recorders, fax, and copying machines. These new devices have enormously speeded up the dissemination of new work from place to place within the United States, from Europe and other continents to the United States, and from the States out to the world. About these I shall say more below.

The triumph of theory is to a considerable degree to be defined as a response to the new social, demographic, and technological situation I have described and as an attempt to think one's way out of it. The teacher wants to be justified in what he or she does. The appeal to theory is one way of seeking that justification. To put this another way, one of the major functions of literary theory is as a critique of ideology, that is, a critique of the taking of a linguistic reality for a material one. The ideology in question in this case includes the hidden (but ideology is by definition hidden) assumptions of our procedures of teaching literature and of the general institutionalization of literary study.

Another way to put this is to say that literary theory is not simply 'theoretical', in the ordinary sense of that word. The function of theory is to produce new readings of literature or other cultural signs: film,

---

3. This is true in spite of the evident excellence of English literature. But Japanese, Chinese, African, and Latin American literature are also of high quality. Many American citizens would have more reasons of cultural inheritance to study these than to read English literature. Even the discipline of American literature is becoming multilingual. The centre of literary study in the immediate future will be new forms of comparative literature, forms very different from the traditional one, for example in a new stress on reading in the original languages.

television, advertising, and so on. These readings are not just additions to knowledge. They are also, or ought to be, 'performative' (see Austin, 1975). The readings sponsored by theory enter into culture to change it. The attempt to contain theory by making it into a topic of study like others is a form of the resistance to theory. This resistance, however, is an intrinsic part of theory itself. Insofar as theory is constative, as its etymological connection with 'seeing' suggests, it adds to the knowledge that it is the historic mission of the university to produce. Insofar as theory is performative, its function is not to add knowledge but to inaugurate change in the historical and material world. These two aspects of theory, the cognitive and the performative, cannot be reconciled. They are an asymmetrical division within theory itself. The knowledge and the performance cannot be related as a logical or dialectical opposition. The cognition to which theoretical reflection leads does not indicate the 'political' uses to which that knowledge should be put, and the performative power of theory may go against what the knowledge gained by it would seem to suggest ought to be its result.

How is this problematic 'triumph of theory' related to new technological developments? As I write this in the early weeks of 1990 I am persuaded that we are on the threshold of enormous transformations both in cultural practices and in their understanding through theory and reading. Such understanding will also help bring about the transformations. Rapid technological changes are moving us all out of the Gutenberg era into an era of multimedia, 'hypertext' or 'hypermedia', a mixing of alphabetic, iconic, and auditory signs. These new technologies are already transforming both the cultures we study and our ways of studying them, including even our ways of studying the literature of the past.

Let me try to explain this in a little more detail, in its relation to the 'triumph of theory'. The recent transformation of literary study, especially the shift to theory, is related in a complex way to the manifold technological changes that have put us all inside what Derrida calls a new 'technological regime of telecommunications' (Derrida, 1981). This relation is not to be defined according to a causal paradigm. The triumph of theory has not been caused by the computer, nor has the shift to theory caused the development of new technological devices, for example new sorts of software. Both the theory and the technology are associated with large-scale social, technological, and institutional changes that have already much altered research, teaching, and writing in literature. They seem certain to change these even more in the next few years.

It is impossible in a brief paper to do more than sketch the ways the computer and associated technologies have already altered research and teaching in literature and will alter it even more in the near future. At first it might seem that the personal computer is no more than an extremely efficient typewriter, but this would be a naive error. The personal computer, the proliferating software developed for it, modems, rapidly expanding databases, laser videos, CD-ROMs, and CDIs (Compact Discs Interactive), have transformed the conditions of authorship, have made copyright laws obsolete, and have turned the printed book into what Richard Lanham calls the 'electronic book' (Lanham, 1989,90). This new form of book will rapidly replace or ought to replace the traditional textbooks used in literature courses. It exists in digitalized form. This means it combines or can combine alphabetic, iconic, and auditory signs—music, word, and picture combined. It is unfixed, constantly in revision. It is likely no longer to have a single author but to be the product of collaboration among many authors connected by an instantaneous network that may cross oceans and link continents, for example by 'Bitnet'. It is no longer 'published' at all in the old sense of hard copy manufacture. Such a 'book' is interactive. The user who calls it up on the screen may alter it, use any part of it separately, expand it or contract it. Each element in it can lead to an indefinitely long trail of references and connections that no longer exist as footnote references but as actual text, pictures, or sounds that can be called up and sorted by searching techniques that are becoming more and more sophisticated, even in software that is practically free, like Macintosh Hypercard.

This new form of 'book' and new form of study, teaching, reading, and research in what it hardly seems appropriate any longer to call simply 'literature' are developments parallel to the dissemination of a worldwide popular culture of film, animation, television, videos, CD players, and various forms of electronic music. An excellent example of this 'electronic book' is the project by Donald Ross and Austin Meredith at the University of Minnesota for an ambitious database combining auditory, visual, and alphabetic material for the study of Thoreau. This ambitious project will initially be developed on a NeXT computer. It will put at a scholar's fingertips a full variorum of Thoreau's works, with the full texts side by side, a large selection of the secondary work on Thoreau, as well as a great assortment of historical materials, graphic and auditory as well as textual data. The project will be a 'scholar's workstation' for advanced research on Thoreau. This will differentiate it from computer environments for undergraduate instruction in literature and art history, like the IRIS project at Brown University. These two ways of using the computer for instruction and research in the humanities seem likely to proliferate rapidly during the next decade, as more and more powerful computers are made available at prices putting them in reach of the student and scholar.

These new technologies are, it can be seen, already radically changing the way we study and understand the literature and other art forms of the past. We now see the past differently. Another example is our relatively recent recognition that Victorian novels, with their tipped-in illustrations, are a multimedia form. Another case is the brilliant demonstration by Nicholas Royle in a forthcoming book that literature in the West has always been a discursive form whose basic assumption is telepathic communication like that given material form in a computer network. A final example is the identification by Jacques Derrida within the work of Hegel, Kant, Nietzsche, Mallarmé, Freud, and others of strange multi-dimensional hypertexts rather than the linear philosophical or poetic argumentations they have traditionally been assumed to be.

The new technologies have reinforced radically new ways of reading or, it would be better to say, powerful renewals of old rhetorical ways of reading. Derrida's *Glas*, *La vérité en peinture*, and *La carte postale* (Derrida, 1974, 1978, 1980) were not written on the computer. Nevertheless, with their complex typography, their punctuation by graphic illustrations, their mixture of different languages and stylistic decorums, their improvised and sometimes explicitly dated diary form, and their disquieting use of unconventional dialogue technique, as if an indefinite number of different voices or rather different powers of writing were competing to get themselves down on paper, they invoke ways of 'writing' that have been made technologically available now to anyone with a personal computer, especially to anyone with a Macintosh.[4] Richard Lanham has called the personal computer the 'ultimate postmodern work of art' (Lanham, 1990, p.37). *Glas* and the personal computer appeared at more or less the same time. Both work

---

4. It would be an error to underestimate the resistance of the university to these changes. As Derrida (1983) says: "The reproductive force of authority can get along... comfortably with declarations or theses whose content presents itself as revolutionary provided that they respect the rites of legitimation, the rhetoric and institutional symbolism which defuses and neutralizes whatever comes from outside the system. What is unacceptable is what, underlying positions or theses, upsets this deeply entrenched contract, the order of these norms, and which does so in the very *form* of works, of teaching or of writing."

selfconsciously and deliberately to make obsolete the traditional codex linear book and to replace it with the new multilinear multimedia hypertext that is rapidly becoming the characteristic mode of expression both in culture and in the study of cultural forms.

The 'triumph of theory' in literary studies and the transformation of such studies by the digital revolution are aspects of the same sweeping changes. The recent overthrow of repressive regimes in Eastern Europe and the worldwide unification of the financial markets into one immense network are but other aspects of these transformations. The term 'global village' no longer seems adequate to name the new situation, unless one stresses that it is an ironic oxymoron for an unheard-of form of conglomeration that as yet has no proper name.

One important aspect of these new technologies of expression and research is political. These technologies are inherently democratic and transnational. They will help create new and hitherto unimagined forms of democracy, political involvement, obligation, and power. The new CD-ROM and DVI (Digital Video Interactive) databases will put a major research library mixing video, sound, graphics, and text at the disposal of students even in junior colleges, or indeed in the hands of people altogether outside our academic institutions. Unprecedented and unpredictable new forms of imaginative scholarship and creativity are almost certain to result from the new technologies. In fact they are already appearing, for example in extremely sophisticated new comic books that exploit the graphics or superimposed windows, or in the proliferation of software designed to exploit the new possibilities.

Those new forms of democracy I have mentioned are not some utopian hope. They are appearing at the moment I write this all over the world, for example in the extraordinary events of the past few months in Eastern Europe, or in the democracy movement in the People's Republic of China, surely destined ultimately to triumph, though no doubt in unforeseen ways, or even in South Africa, where 'sweeping changes' have just been announced and where Nelson Mandela has just been set free at last. These events have been facilitated if not necessitated by the new communications technologies, the transistor radios, for example, that are available to Chinese peasants, or the video cassettes that have played a role in the recent revolutions in Eastern Europe. Far from being necessarily the instruments of thought control, as Orwell in *1984* foresaw, the new regime of telecommunications seems to be inherently democratic. It has helped bring down dictator after dictator in the past few months.

In this new and as yet not definable global economy we are entering, made one world by these new technologies, the isolated monolingual study of single national literatures will soon seem as outmoded as old-fashioned nationalisms themselves. Such study must be replaced by multilingual and multi-ethnic disciplines of collective research and teaching. These new disciplines are as yet hardly imagined, like the new world we are entering. They will borrow from anthropology and studies of popular culture as much as those disciplines have borrowed from literary theory. That new transnational democracy, whatever it will be like, must be based on the recognition and enhancement of cultural and individual differences. Here so-called 'deconstructionisms' in their many forms will play an indispensable role. A constant focus of Derrida's work, for example, has been on heterogeneity in cultural forms, on the idiomatic in signature or text, and on what he calls the 'invention of the other'. 'Invention' here means both creation and discovery, both making up and fortuitous coming upon, as if by chance. The new technologies make such encounters universal. Far from necessarily leading to homogeneity, they give us new ways to preserve and enhance the differences among us that must be a central feature of the new democracy.

References

Austin, J.L. (1975) **How to Do Things with Words**, 2nd edn. Cambridge, Mass: Harvard University Press (1st edn, 1962).

de Man, P. (1986) **The Resistance to Theory**. Minneapolis: University of Minnesota Press.

Derrida, J. (1974) **Glas**. Paris: Galilée. English translation: Glas, translated by J. Leavey and R. Rand. Lincoln and London: University of Nebraska Press, 1986.

Derrida, J. (1978) **La vérité en peinture**. Paris: Flammarion. English translation: **The Truth in Painting**, translated by G. Bennington and I. McLeod. Chicago: University of Chicago Press, 1987.

Derrida, J. (1980) **La carte postale**. Paris: Aubier-Flammarion. English translation: **The Post Card**, translated by A. Bass. Chicago: University of Chicago Press, 1987.

Derrida, J. (1981) Télépathie. **Furor**, February 1981, 5- 41.

Derrida, J. (1983) The time of a thesis: punctuations. Translated by K.

McLaughline. In **Philosophy in France Today**, edited by A. Montefiore, pp. 34-50. Cambridge: Cambridge University Press.

Lanham, R. (1989) The electronic word: literary study and the digital revolution. **New Literary History**, 20, 265-290.

Lanham, R. (1990) The extraordinary convergence: democracy, technology, theory, and the university curriculum. **South Atlantic Quarterly**, 89, 27-50.

Leitch, V.B. (1988) **American Literary Criticism from the Thirties to the Eighties.** New York: Columbia University Press.

Macksey, R. and Donato, E. (1970) **The Languages of Criticism and the Sciences of Man.** Baltimore: Johns Hopkins University Press.

Miller, J.H. (1987) The triumph of theory, the resistance to reading, and the question of the material base. **PMLA**, 102, 281- 291.

Technology and Linguistics Research

Antonio Zampolli

Instituto di Linguistica Computationale, Pisa

1 Introductory remarks

Whereas in most of the humanities the computer is considered essentially as a powerful tool which can assist researchers in their traditional disciplinary activities, in linguistics the computational approach has given rise to a new discipline, computational linguistics. This seems to me the single major specific impact of the computer in the field of linguistics.

2 The formation of computational linguistics and its relationship to literary and linguistic computing

When[5] the use of electronic data processing techniques began to be directed to linguistics data at the end of the 1940s, two main lines of research were activated quite independently:

- Machine Translation (MT), and

- Lexical Text Analysis (LTA: production of indices, concordances, frequency counts, etc.).

While MT was promoted mainly in 'hard-science' departments, LTA was developed mainly in humanities departments. For this reason there was very little contact between the two.

Although at the beginning of the 1960s, there was some recognition of a possible reciprocal interest in topics such as text encoding systems for different alphabets, frequency-counts of linguistic elements in large corpora, and automated dictionaries, real cooperation was very rare, if

---

5. This paragraph is extracted, in part, from Calzolari and Zampolli, 1991.

not totally absent. After 1966 the two fields diverged still further. The year 1966 was particularly important for both lines of research, but for opposing reasons. The Prague International Conference 'Les Machines dans la Linguistique' ratified the international acceptance of LTA as an autonomous disciplinary field, and its extension to a broader area, which included new dimensions of processing (phonology, historical linguistics, dialectology, etc.), called Literary and Linguistic Computing (LLC).

Around the same period, the use of computers spread to other humanities disciplines. Joseph Raben founded the journal *Computers in the Humanities* in 1966. The computational processing of large texts has characterized from the very beginning most humanistic computer-assisted projects, so that some researchers recognize a subfield of 'computers in the humanities' (text processing for the humanities: TPH), which utilizes the traditional tools of LLC (indices, concordances, textual database access, etc.) for retrieving and analyzing factual information referred to in the text.

In the very same years in which LLC and TPH gained ground, the well-known ALPAC report (1966) brought to a sudden stop the majority of MT projects in the world, and marked the beginning of the so-called 'dark ages' of MT. Following, *de facto*, the recommendations of the ALPAC report, basic research on natural language processing slowly occupied the area characterized so far by MT activities, and emerged as a new disciplinary activity, computational linguistics (CL).

In spite of ALPAC recommendations for research on large-scale grammars, dictionaries, and corpora, CL focused mainly on the development of methods for the utilization of formal linguistic models in the analysis and generation of isolated sentences, in an almost exclusively monolingual framework, and at the grammatical level. It almost completely neglected the development of lexica, which were effectively restricted to small toy-lexicons of a few dozen words. A distorted (I believe) interpretation of the Chomskyan paradigm led to an almost complete lack of interest in corpora and quantitative data, which were attracting much attention in the LLC area partly due to projects for national historical dictionaries and for frequency dictionaries.

On the other hand, LLC and TPH also delayed in taking advantage of the know-how, methodology, and tools produced from the very beginning by MT in the field of automatic lexica. Not only had MT developed research on specialized hardware, storage, access techniques, inflectional and derivational morphological analysis, but certain projects had already begun the collection of large sets of monolingual and bilingual lexical and terminological data. Very few exceptions can be reported in the LLC field, all primarily motivated by attempts to automate the lemmatization of texts for the production of lemmatized indices and concordances. The first experiments are related to Latin (CAAL, Gallarate, and LASLA, Liège).

For several years practically no relationship existed between LLC/TPH and CL. As local organizer of the 1973 Pisa COLING, I endeavoured to include in the call for papers, and to promote in the Conference, sections explicitly dedicated to topics which could delineate the areas of common interest. The attempt was successful in terms of joint participation, and it was probably not just by chance that Joan Smith presented there, at an international level, the newly founded ALLC (Smith, 1973). But in the 1970s a (so to speak) 'purist' approach characterized the general reflections of CL, which was searching for a definitional and a disciplinary identity, focusing on problems of computation and on the nature of the algorithmic procedures, rather than on the nature of the results and on linguistic, in particular textual, data. The variety of points of view is exemplified in the *Foreword* by Karlgren, and in the *Introduction* by Zampolli, to the *Proceedings* of COLING 1973 (Zampolli and Calzolari, 1973).

The development of CL, in the following years, was influenced by the interest in Natural Language Processing (NLP) shown by large sectors of Artificial Intelligence. Many efforts were directed towards the study of methods and tools for prototypes performing a 'deep understanding' of natural language, necessarily limited to restricted linguistic fragments and to 'miniature' pragmatic subdomains, thus enlarging the gap between CL and LLC/TPH activities.

In the LLC framework, the attention of a large part of the research community was captured by the new technological developments, and efforts were directed towards mastering new hardware and software facilities: the increasing variety of rich sets of characters, OCR, photocomposition, large database techniques, personal computers, new storage media, general purpose editors and wordprocessors, standardized concordance packages, etc.

Only in the last two years has a variety of contributing factors started to arouse the reciprocal interest of people working both in CL and LLC/TPH. Increasing contacts and exchanges, joint organization of conferences or conference sections, and cooperative projects formulated at the international level are all external signs of this process.

This convergence is partly due to the activities of some Institutes, with programmes of research in both fields, and thus naturally operating to construct a bridge and to promote synergies. However, in my opinion, the key fact is that both fields now recognize that an important aspect of their development depends on the capability of processing, at least at some level of linguistic analysis, large quantities of 'real' texts of various types. It seems to me that these trends characterize the actual 'Zeitgeist', and will be examined in further detail in section 5.

3 Computational linguistics: methodologies and results

Since[6] the first machine translation projects of the early 1950s, considerable effort has been devoted to the study and development of methods for the analysis and generation of natural languages. The reasons are both theoretical and practical.

1. At the 'scientific level': testing grammars and rules proposed by linguistic theories; studying and developing formalisms for representing morphological, syntactic, semantic, pragmatic knowledge; accumulating and assessing large formalized descriptions of natural languages; constructing models of the psychological processing of language understanding and of language users; etc.

2. At the 'applicative level': to develop linguistic components for specific systems, oriented to practical industrial and commercial applications, which involve the automatic processing of natural languages (NLP).

3.1 Analysis
Most effort has been directed to processing individual sentences. We can say that the overall objective of sentence analysis, roughly speaking, is to determine what a 'sentence' means. In practice, this usually involves translating the natural language input into a language (e.g. formal logic) which can be 'interpreted' by computer programs. The analysis usually

---

6. This paragraph is extracted, in part, from a survey prepared by the author for the European Science Foundation, in cooperation with S. Hockey.

involves components at the morphological, syntactic, lexical and semantic levels, which can intervene in sequence, or can be activated in turn by a supervisor, or can work in parallel.

3.1.1 Morphological analysis

Morphological analyzers usually try to decompose graphical words into an invariant string (i.e. the part which remains constant in all the inflected forms of a lemma) and inflectional endings. The recognition of endings provides the description of the morphosyntactical properties of the word: part of speech, gender, number, tense, person, etc. The invariant string is normally used as an access key to the computational lexicon of the system, to obtain, from the relevant entry, the associated linguistic information on the syntactic and semantic properties of the word. Some analyzers try to recognize, in addition to the inflectional endings, also the affixes. In this case, the system tries to decompose the word into '(prefix) base (suffix)*, ending', and the access key to the lexicon is the 'base'. In a certain sense, we can say that those systems include a formal representation of the derivational morphology. The two level morphology model deserves special mention (Koskenniemi, 1983).

3.1.2 Computational lexicon

A computational lexicon is a collection of lexical entries, properly structured and stored in a form easily accessible by computer. Each entry consists of two parts:

1. The head: a specific string of characters which is matched to locate a particular lexical entry (see the previous section).

2. Information on the linguistic properties of the lexical entry. Typical examples are: the canonical form (lemma); part of speech; inflectional paradigm; number, form, and selectional restrictions of the arguments; semantic features; semantic relations with other entries (e.g. synonyms) or within a conceptual structure (e.g. taxonomy).

The form of the syntactic and semantic information stored in each entry usually depends on the requirements of the grammar and the semantic analyzer of the specific NLP system associated with the lexicon. When used in association with a concordance program, a computational lexicon can suggest the lemmatization of the words. Of course, if a word is homographic, two or more lemmata are proposed, and usually the researcher will choose among them, with or without the help of the computer.

3.1.3 Syntactic component

The syntactic analysis component basically performs two functions.

The first function determines the syntactical structure of the input sentence. For example, it identifies the various phrases, their functions (subject, object, predicate), etc. This is more often done by assigning a tree-structure to the input. The analysis is performed by an algorithm which applies a set of formal syntactic rules (the 'grammar') to the sentence, starting from the information provided by the lexical look-up for each word.

The most used grammatical formalism has been the so-called 'Augmented Phrase Structure Grammar'. Several algorithms are now available, and their computational properties are well understood. Several difficult problems are instead associated with parsers based on transformational grammars. The Augmented Transition Network Model (ATN), introduced by Woods in 1970, has been established as one of the standard tools in computational linguistics. It is particularly suited to write small, efficient, syntactically oriented systems. CHART, (based on work by Kay, 1973, and Kaplan, 1973) is a very powerful data structure for parsing, providing a very general framework for representing input, output and intermediate results in all sorts of linguistic data processing.

In recent years, various new syntactic formalisms have emerged, both as a reaction to, and as a continuation of the Chomskyan paradigm, which have in common the utilization, in a principled way, of the unification mechanism: Lexical Functional Grammars (Bresnan, 1982), Generalized Phrase Structure Grammars (Gazdar *et al*, 1985), Head-driven phase structure Grammar (Pollard *et al*, 1987), etc.. It is important to note that these new trends pervade both theoretical and computational linguistics at the same time, and have emerged in contexts where linguists and computational linguists cooperate, almost without distinction. Another trend is that of restricting the role of syntax in favour of the lexical component.

The second function of syntactic analysis is to 'regularize' the syntactic structure. Various types of structures are mapped into a smaller number of simple canonical structures, thus simplifying subsequent processing. Those structures are often intended to represent the functional relationships among the various phrases within a sentence. The verbal element is usually the focus around which the other phrases revolve.

3.1.4 Semantic component
The major aims of semantic components are:

1. To disambiguate ambiguous syntactic structures

2. To disambiguate homographic or polysemic words

3. To determine the 'general meaning of a sentence'.

The structure produced by the syntactic component is usually mapped into a formal language, which is designed to be unambiguous and to have simple rules for interpretation and inference. In practical systems, the 'meaning' of a sentence is, roughly speaking, what we want the system to do in response to our input: retrieve data, direct a robot, etc. In general, this means translating the natural language input into the formal language of the database retrieval system, of a robot command system, etc. Within the paradigm of formal logic, both propositional and predicate logic are used.

Selectional restrictions are often used for disambiguation. If one of the competing structures, produced by the syntax, violates a selectional restriction constraint, it is rejected as semantically anomalous. For example, a verb can be 'restricted' in the range of items it can accept as subjects, objects, etc. A structure is rejected if the proposed subject is not a member of the accepted class. Preference semantic (e.g. Wilks, 1975) analyzers do not reject structures. They merely 'prefer' some to others. In this way, for example, slightly non-standard subjects and objects can be allowed, so accepting 'non-literal' uses. Ambiguity is resolved by selecting the most preferred readings.

Significant generalizations can be made concerning how noun phrases are semantically related to the verbs and to the adjectives in a sentence. The most influential work for computational approaches has been case grammar (Fillmore, 1968) and its successors and modifications (Bruce, 1975).

Already during the '60s, work in cognitive psychology and artificial intelligence has developed a type of structure known as a semantic network for representing 'meaning'. These networks are graphs made up of nodes, which generally represent a word-meaning, and links between the nodes which reflect the relationships among the nodes (for an overview see Woods, 1975).

Various conceptual analyzers are based on a common semantic representation, called 'conceptual dependency' network (developed originally by R. Schank (1975)). Basically the action, normally referred to by the verb, is represented as a conceptual skeleton, consisting of 'primitive acts' (selected in a short list), which has a fixed number of 'slots' (e.g. the 'actor', the 'object', the 'direction': from-to), to be filled by items appearing in the input sentence. The analyzer tries to 'discover' compatible fillers for each slot.

Disambiguating and interpreting a sentence requires more than just linguistic knowledge. It also involves accessing knowledge of the world, general or domain-specific, and of the specific characteristics of the communicative context (dialogue, etc.). The distinction between linguistic and pragmatic knowledge is known to be very difficult. A great deal of effort is being directed at a cooperation between computational linguistics, artificial intelligence and cognitive science, to study appropriate methods for representing and using knowledge.

A knowledge representation, in its more general sense, is any framework in which information about language and the world can be stored and retrieved. While there is a wide range of knowledge representation formalism, all share common properties. Knowledge representation systems can be thought of as being made up of two distinct parts: the knowledge base (KB), which is the set of data structures that store the information, and the inference engine, which provides a set of operations on the knowledge base (Allen, 1987, p.315 ff.).

KL-ONE is a language which is used extensively for research into problems of understanding natural language and knowledge representation (Schmolze and Brachmann, 1982). It is based on the representation of general concepts (classes of individuals), individual concepts (instantiations of general concepts), and of the relations between concepts. A general concept is part of conceptual taxonomy, in which it inherits the properties of the superordinates. An appropriate formalism allows the description of the 'internal structure' of a concept: e.g. the parts of the concept (which are in turn concepts) and their functional relations within the structure of the concept. Appropriate mechanisms use the knowledge to make inferences.

3.15 Discourse component
Much more is known about the processing of individual sentences than about the determination of discourse structure, despite the fact that the

resolution of ambiguities in individual sentences in certain cases (e.g. pronouns) presupposes the ability 'to understand' the connections between sentences.

There have been a number of efforts to define conditions which must be satisfied for a text to be coherent. This work, carried on mainly in the framework of text linguistics, has shown that text analysis will depend critically on the ability to organize relevant world knowledge and make substantial inferencing. Much of the recent research focuses on methods of organizing knowledge for processing new data.

Several approaches use 'frames'. A 'prototype frame' describes, with a set of labelled 'slots', properties, constituents and participants of a class of objects or static situations. When a frame is activated, the parts of the frame specify what kind of information needs to be found in the discourse for a situation to be understable (Minsky, 1975).

'Scripts' are designed to capture the typical knowledge of speakers about a stereotyped sequence of events. A script enables the storage of an outline of a certain type of 'episode', providing the capability of predicting activities, actors, and objects which can be assumed to be present, even if they are not referred to in the input, thus allowing inferences, disambiguations, and connections (Schank, Abelson, 1977).

'Plans' are used to analyze descriptions of a novel sequence of events. A plan consists of a goal, alternative sequences of actions for achieving the goal, and preconditions to apply a given sequence. 'To construct a casual chain for a novel sequence, a means-end analysis must be performed; that is, we must try "to understand" how later events in a text act to further previously stated goals'. (Grishmann, 1986i; Wilensky, 1981).

3.2 Generation

The task of generating language has been undertaken mainly for two kinds of purposes:

1. To test grammars proposed by theoretical linguists. Because of the complex interactions possible, it is desirable to use the computer to verify that a proposed set of rules actually works. The Friedman (1971) Transformational Grammar Tester generated sentences in accordance with a proposed transformational grammar, so that linguists could verify that their grammar did, in fact, generate only grammatical sentences.

2. To generate natural language answers for the user of a given computational system, in cases where a pre-compiled list of fixed messages is not sufficient. User acceptance often requires the generation of complex sentences, and even multi-sentence texts. The generation consists of translating a 'meaning' representation into natural language. The typical process goes from a logical representation, through a deep structure, to the sentence.

It is not generally agreed whether a generation system could be obtained by simply reversing the order of the application of the components and the rules of the analysis. In practice, the problems which arise in generation are often different. The difference between collocations ('idioms of encoding') and fixed phrases ('idioms of decoding') is an example.

Generation has been given less effort than analysis. The specific problems of generation have been under-estimated. One of the reasons is that, whereas an analyzer should be able to accept and recognize many paraphrases of the same information or command from the user, it will suffice to generate only one of these forms. Furthermore, analysis has to deal with the ambiguities present in the texts.

4 Computational linguistics and linguistics

4.1 *Grammatical formalisms*
Grammar is the field in which interactions have been more intense between linguistics and CL, despite the different purposes of the two disciplines.[7]

Much of the work that led to the development of new grammatical formalisms grew out of an attempt to overcome the difficulties of applying the formalism of transformational grammars in parsing.

This work has been performed from different starting points, but

---

7. Whereas in generative linguistics the emphasis was mainly on the formalisms by which linguistic descriptions can be specified (both in the form of constructive rules which define the range of possible structures and in the form of constraints on the possible allowable structures), and in claims about the nature of language implicit in that formalism, computational linguistics has pursued the goal of specifying a theory to such a level of detail and completeness that computer programs based on it can be written which analyze and generate natural languages.

several approaches make substantial use of *features*, and *functions*, and are influenced by the notion of *cases*.

The creation of *Lexical Functional Grammar* (Bresnan, 1982) is perhaps the best well-known example of a methodological and theoretical new development due to the interaction of linguists and computational linguists.[8] It is an attempt to solve problems that arise in transformational and in ATN grammars by using *additive descriptions*.

Other types of grammars, designed in the CL context, include for example *definite clause grammar* (Colmerauer, 1978), *slot grammar* (McCord, 1980), *functional unification grammar* (Kay, 1985), *head-driven phrase structure grammar* (Pollard and Sag, 1987), etc.

4.2 The generative and the computational paradigms

During the second half of the 1970s, a computational paradigm (the term is used here in the sense of Kuhn, 1970) was proposed for linguistic research, as opposed to, or at least considerably different from the generative paradigm, in those days dominant in theoretical linguistics.

The computational paradigm views the language as a communicative process based on knowledge. The task of the linguist should consist in understanding the organization of this process and the structure of knowledge.

> Our metaphor is that of computation, as we understand it from our experience with *stored program digital computers*. The computer shares with the human mind the ability to manipulate symbols and carry out complex processes that include making decisions on the basis of stored knowledge. Unlike the human mind, the computer's workings are completely open to inspection and study, and we can experiment by building programs and knowledge bases to our specifications. Theoretical concepts of *program* and *data* can form the basis for building precise computational models of mental processing. (Winograd, 1983).

In this approach, CL is nearly identified with theoretical linguistics *tout-court*.

---

8. As an example of the interactions between CL and linguistics, I think it would be interesting to trace the history of CL in the Bay area, which also represents a substantial part of the history of CL.

Computational linguists are not simply linguists who have found ways of avoiding some of the labour that their trade would otherwise force upon them by consigning it to a machine. There are linguists who have found, or who hope to find, something in the metaphors and theories of computing that reflects in a fundamental way on the human linguistic faculty. (Kay, 1982).

One should look to computers for fundamental insight into human language because computers are the only devices we have to embody a notion of abstract symbolic processing.

Computers are, as Alan Newell is fond of saying, the only semiotic engines we have. It is to them that we must look for the parts out of which convincing psychological models of linguistic performance will be built. (Kay, 1982).

In this way, the basic goals of linguistics largely coincide with those of psycholinguistics, and the differences reside in the experimental tools. Computational linguistics *and* linguistics are considered as a part of cognitive science.

An intense debate on the differences between the linguistic paradigm, as represented by the generative-transformational school, and the computational linguistic paradigm appeared in a series of papers in *Cognition* in 1976-77 (Dresher and Hornstein, 1976, 1977a, 1977b; Schank and Abelson, 1977; Winograd, 1977).

Both paradigms recognize, as a basic task, the study of the structure of the knowledge processed by an individual who uses a language and, as a basic principle, the hypothesis that this knowledge can be understood as formal rules concerning the structure of symbols (Winograd, 1983i). But major differences exist.

The generative paradigm recognizes two aspects in language: *competence*, an abstract characterization of a speaker's knowledge; and *performance*, the processes that actually determine what a speaker says or how an utterance is understood in a particular context. But, as a matter of fact, the study of performance is practically ignored. The structure of a person's linguistic competence is characterized independently of any process by which it is manifested. 'The performance component is seen as theoretically secondary to the independent specification of competence' (Winograd, 1983). Furthermore, most researchers have adopted the 'autonomy of syntax hypothesis': there would be relatively independent bodies of phenomena that can be characterized by syntactic rules without considering other aspects of language or thought.

In the computational paradigm, instead, the organization of the processes of comprehension and production play a central role. As a consequence, particular attention is given to the interaction between linguistic and non-linguistic knowledge, and to how linguistic acts fit into a larger context of action and knowledge.

But the debate between the two paradigms has progressively cooled down for several reasons. It has been recognized that the present state of knowledge about natural language processing is so preliminary that the attempt to build a cognitively correct model (i.e. a computational analogue of the human processing mechanism in language production and comprehension) is not feasible.

'Before researchers can begin a project to build such a model, there would have to be simultaneous major advances in both computational linguistics and the experimental techniques used by psycholinguists' (Allen, 1987i). The current goal is, instead, 'a comprehensive, computational theory of language understanding and production that is well-defined and linguistically motivated' (Allen, 1987). Constructing such a computational theory would be a first preparatory step in producing a cognitively correct theory.

Even if for the moment the ambition of constructing cognitive models has been postponed, the production of this computational theory seems to be a very long-term research programme, and CL needs to explore the entire process of language understanding and generation.

A major problem is to overcome the present phase in which isolated attempts lead to the continuous appearance of new, rapidly abandoned proposals. It is necessary to move to a stage in which it will be possible to build on the outcome of previous research.

This seems to me also a necessary condition to draw linguists' attention to the specific problems which CL was the first to raise: for example, the construction of knowledge representation formalisms which can support semantic analyses of sentences; modelling of reasoning processes that account for the way in which context, both textual and extralinguistic, affects the interpretation of sentences; generalizations on the meaning differentiation of polysemous words; discourse structures of various text-types (narrative, dialogue); strategies for semantic interpretation, etc.

In this way we shall perhaps come closer to making it possible, as forecast by Charles Fillmore in 1977 'for workers in linguistic semantics, cognitive psychology, and artificial intelligence—and maybe even language philosophy—to talk to each other using more or less the same language, and thinking about more or less the same problems'.

A new paradigm, *connectionism*, seems to call for the attention of CL. But it seems to me too early to try to evaluate the possible impact of connectionism, through the mediation of CL, on linguistics, even if the first signs of interest are already appearing, in particular in psycholinguistics.

5 Current trends and possible developments

5.1 CL and language industries

The need to consolidate and progressively build on partial achievements has become even more urgent in the light of the increasing interest of national and international public authorities and private companies for the technical, economic, and social potentialities of the field of the so-called 'language industries' (LI).[9]

This expression, coined on the occasion of a Congress sponsored by the Council of Europe in Tours in February 1986, is used to indicate activities based on computational systems, oriented to practical industrial and commercial applications, which contain, as an essential part, natural language processing components. Examples of typical applications include, within the domain of speech technology: access control, command and control to data entry, driver stations, document creation, telephone enquiries, transaction processing by telephone, database enquiry, environmental control, voice messaging, announcement systems, augmented communication for handicapped people, etc. For written texts, we can quote: spelling checkers, computer-assisted lexicography and terminology, natural language interfaces, machine translation, information retrieval, computer-assisted language learning and teaching, computer-assisted consultation of reference works, translator workstations, etc.

A set of different factors and conditions are requiring today the

---

9.   From the early times of machine translation, the perspective applications of linguistic theories have gained financial support for linguistics, in particular in the USA, where the selection of particular lines of research for support has been strongly influenced by intended computer applications.

promotion and development of LI. The key is, in my opinion, the advent of the so-called 'information society'. The global dimension of the economy conceived as a worldwide system, together with the techno-logical development of telecommunications systems, entails a growing information flow. The principal information vehicles are still natural languages, for both the production and the storing tasks. Furthermore, the major part of the information in natural language is nowadays produced directly through computer use, and recorded on machine-read-able media: wordprocessors, office automation, electronic mail, photo-composition, databases, etc. Various countries are considering the possibility of progressively recording entire libraries in machine-read-able form.

This situation puts an obvious pressure for the creation of new products and services for the various economic activities primarily involved in information handling. The following passage of Makoto Nagao (1989) seems particularly relevant:

> Computers are a fusion with and unification of communications technology at both the hardware and the software levels, and computer systems will undoubtedly enter every corner of future society. When that day arrives, the most important technology will be specifically concerned with neither hardware nor software, but with what I have been advocating for many years: 'information-ware'. In other words, the central problem will regard the ways in which the information signals sent by human beings will be mech-anically processed, transmitted, stored, and then recalled in a form which can be interpreted by other human beings. The essence of informationware is therefore how information can be efficiently stored in a computer and activated in response to the various demands of its users. Information can in fact take different forms, including writing, speech and visual images, but objectively, the most accurate means for transmitting and receiving information is writing. For this reason, of the various aspects of informationware, linguistic information and its processing technique will be the primary technology at the heart of the information society. Such technology might be called 'language engineering', and the indus-try which it will span will be the 'language industry'.

A central aspect of the language industry is multilingualism. Only an 'elite' minority in the world can operate today in a foreign language, without sacrificing its performance (Perschke, 1988). Furthermore, the conservation of national languages, a principle adopted from the beginning, for example, by the EC, is an important condition for the preservation of national cultural identities.

The need for monolingual and multilingual natural language processing systems, to be used in products for information handling in the LI framework, is uncontroversial. Some studies are carried out in order to narrow down and focus the most urgent tasks and targets, identifying the principal sectors of activities and their economic dimension.

It seems urgent to evaluate the present state of the art in linguistic research and engineering, and the possibilities of large-scale development, in particular:—which products can be created on the basis of existing technologies;—which applications can be envisaged at short and medium terms;—which are the priority areas and tasks for linguistic basic and applied research;—which can be an appropriate research and development strategy;—by which measures, at the organizational level, the public authorities and professional scientific associations can stimulate progress in the field.

In this framework, one of the priority needs, recognized by several researchers in various countries, is a description of natural language, in a form which is suitable for computer use, performed as far as possible exhaustively, at least for those linguistic aspects which can be treated at the present state-of-the-art linguistics and natural language processing. Such extended descriptions are considered the bases for the construction of 'robust' components capable of dealing with the various types of large real texts which are the typical objects of a wide range of LI applications already possible or foreseeable at short and medium term.

These descriptions concern, first of all, grammars and lexica, and can take the form of repositories of grammatical and lexical knowledge bases. Large corpora of textual material in the form of textual databases are considered essential sources of information.

5.2 The impact of current needs on research priorities and directions
I shall now consider how the need for robust NLP components and for the consolidation of linguistic knowledge description are interrelated, and which directions are likely to be taken in CL and linguistics research, in order to try to satisfy those needs.

5.2.1 *Robust NLP components*

The recognition of lexical units and syntactic structures is needed by all language industry applications. But the humanistic disciplines will also benefit from robust analyzers, capable of dealing, at some syntactic level, with large quantities and varieties of texts.

Linguistics. Different linguistic schools assign various theoretical status to (spoken and written) texts: results of performance acts; samples of statistical populations; instantiation of 'la parole'; etc. [10]

Linguists typically interact with texts to construct inventories of linguistic units, to examine syntagmatic behaviour, to discover personal, social, temporal, genre variations. Frequency of use in texts is considered to be the result of voluntary and/or unconscious choices within the range of alternatives offered by the linguistic system, and their variations are connected in various ways to research on performance mechanisms, stylistic habits, and sociolinguistic trends (Halliday, 1990). In compiling reference works (lexica, grammars), linguists collect evidence and examples.

The interaction with texts is obviously more useful if the access keys to the texts include not only strings of textual characters (occurrence and co-occurrence of graphical forms or parts of forms), but also the formal representation of units, structures, and relations, categories identified at various linguistic levels. Until now, computational research on textual corpora has generally been performed only on graphical forms. This is due to the considerable time and high cost required to manually perform the linguistic analysis and to encode its results. The (at least partial) automatization of the analysis operations is a necessary condition if we wish to exploit adequately the growing wealth of textual data which is progressively available in machine-readable form. The structures recognized by the parser can be either 'annotated' (i.e. explicitly represented) in the texts, for subsequent retrieval and access, or directly 'computed' each time by the parser, in performance of specific requests. [11]

---

10. See Zampolli, 1975.
11. A debate is going on at present on the relative merits of the two approaches. See the discussions at the January 1990 SALT Club Workshop on Corpus Linguistics in Oxford.

Text-oriented disciplines (philosophy, stylistics, literary research, etc.). These disciplines will also benefit from the possibility of retrieving, in the texts, explicitly represented linguistic units, possibly in connection with conceptual units, structures, and relations. So-called 'content-analysis' has, from the very beginning, associated information derived from dictionary look-up with words in the texts.

Textual database access systems, produced in CL, now make it possible to search texts for the occurrence or co-occurrence of families of semantically and/or conceptually related 'terms', interactively defined by the researcher, and considered as 'indicators' of themes, motives and, in general, compositive modules. The researcher can also invoke the assistance of structured knowledge sources such as, for example, lexical knowledge bases, in which semantic/conceptual relations among lexical units are explicitly represented: conceptual taxonomies, synonyms, antonyms, etc.[12]

Humanistic disciplines which consider texts as sources of factual information. Linguistic tools can enhance the capabilities of information retrieval systems on large quantities of full texts. Historical and legal researches are obvious examples of disciplines which require information retrieval systems aimed at identifying extralinguistic entities, and their relations referred to in the text. Very often, given the historical distribution of the source texts, the neutralization of diachronic linguistic variants is requested.[13]

The recognition of morphological variations, synonyms, paraphrases, anaphoric references, etc., can help to reduce the 'silence' in the retrieval processes. The solution of lexical and structural ambiguities will help to reduce the 'noise'. The 'conceptual' lexicon can function as a 'thesaurus' of the common core language (Bindi and Calzolari, 1990).

5.2.2 Features of robust components

The use of computers for analyzing texts could be very useful, and even permit new types of research and applications, both in the humanities and in the language industries, even if:

---

12. See as an example the DBT full text database system developed at the ILC in Pisa (Picchi, 1988), and its interaction with lexical knowledge bases (Calzolari and Picchi, 1988).
13. See the SIL system developed in Pisa by Bozzi and Cappelli (1987), which is now connected to the CLIO system.

1. the analysis has not been carried out completely successfully: for example, if some parts of the sentence are not fully analyzed, or if the parser is unable to reach the final level of the structure, but stops with partial, not fully connected, substructures;

2. the computer is requested, not to perform the analysis in a fully automatic way, but only to assist the human operator in performing his tasks.

We need to develop and test 'robust parsers', i.e. parsers capable of:

1. Processing the variety of phenomena occurring in real texts (e.g. repetitions, ellipses, 'agrammaticalities', abbreviated styles), and using large grammars, covering extended subsets of a language.

   For various historical reasons in the last decades, theoretical linguists have relied mainly on introspection and on native speaker intuition. In an effort to evaluate competing syntactic theories, their work has focused on the theoretical properties of their models, concentrating on the explanation of peculiar linguistic phenomena. As a consequence, a large amount of CL research in practice tends to revolve around little toy subsets of artificially constructed linguistic forms. Only a few hope that such systems may be expanded and linked together until they cover the entire language. The grossly unrepresentative nature of such examples is evident. Therefore, their systems fail as soon as they are exposed to genuinely unselected, authentic input. Only the analysis of corpora, constructed in such a way as to represent a realistic variety of text-types, and pragmatic and communicative contexts, can give appropriate insight into the real concrete usages of language, which often elude the attention of theoretical linguists (Garside, Leech and Sampson, 1987).

2. Continuing to work even if they do not reach the intended level of analysis, providing the results of eventual lower level analysis, and presenting unresolved ambiguity in an economical way. Alternatively, they can call for human assistance.

3. Making use also of statistical knowledge, derived from corpus analysis. When natural language is used in specific domains or communicative contexts (sublanguages: e.g. maintenance manuals, weather reports, technical articles for a specific field), it may be restricted in lexical, syntactic, semantic, and discourse properties.

Sometimes it includes peculiar features absent in the general language. In particular, semantic constraints can be enumerated in more detail, and are more strictly respected in the textual use, so that we can expect a significant contribution to the solution of syntactic and lexical ambiguities. It has also been shown that the frequency distribution, in the texts, of specific linguistic units can be related in a characteristic way to specific sublanguages or text-types.

Some of the recent NLP systems, which are most successful in terms of concrete applications for LI, rely strongly on the use of probabilities which are established by observing the frequencies in language corpora. As an example, we can quote, in particular, text to speech, speech recognition, optical character recognition, spelling checkers, linguistic critiquing and, more recently, practically-oriented speech-connected machine-translation prototypes.

4. Having access to large computational lexica. To analyze real texts a computer must recognize thousands of words. The majority of NLP systems have so far concentrated their efforts on grammar development. A recent poll has shown that the average lexicon in NLP projects includes only a few dozen words. Furthermore, each new project usually starts the construction of its lexicon from scratch.

5.3 Reusable linguistic knowledge sources
Robust NLP components thus require that CL creates large grammars, lexica, and textual corpora.

The construction of lexica, grammars, and corpora of adequate size and coverage is a very difficult, expensive, time-consuming task. Therefore, various disciplines (linguistics, CL, AI), are today considering the problem of the re-usability of linguistic knowledge.

5.3.1 Lexica
NLP is based on information about words: what they are, how they sound, how they connect, what they mean.

There is good evidence for the power of [a] dictionary-intensive approach to NLP. Although clever algorithms are also necessary, the quality of [a] broad-coverage NLP program depends mainly on the number of words that it knows about, and the amount that it knows about each one. (Libermann, 1990, personal communication).

Broad-coverage programs, once they exist, serve as important tools in further research; dictionaries themselves, once constructed, serve as data for other research.

Theorists of many persuasions are converging on one form or another of 'lexicalized grammars', in which most syntactic and semantic information is part of the representation of particular words.

The problem of re-usability in computational lexica and in linguistic resources in general has two complementary aspects:

1. It is important to re-use existing data, in particular traditional dictionaries, which now often exist in machine-readable form for photocomposition. Computer assisted procedures can extract not only information which is explicitly formulated, but also information implicitly embedded in the dictionary. For example, a variety of semantic and conceptual relations can be extracted by the definitions: taxonomy, typical subject, 'set of', 'used for', etc. (Calzolari, 1988).

2. New large lexical databases must be multifunctional, i.e. must be re-usable in a variety of applications, to avoid duplication of effort.

The investigation of the feasibility of standardization will concern, first of all, a description of lexical units at various levels of linguistic information and representation formalism. Some levels of description (orthography, phonetics, phonology) are obviously less controversial than others.

Other levels present specific problems.

At the syntagmatic level, recent work in traditional and computational lexicography, but also, among others, in meaning- text-theory, has emphasized the necessity for a description of collocational possibilities of individual lemmas. Knowledge about possible collocations is still very limited. Besides investigating typologies of collocation phenomena, and to what degree a formalization of collocational description is feasible, it appears urgent to design methods and tools to identify and collect data from textual corpora (Bindi and Calzolari, 1990).

The most crucial issue for a description of the syntactic properties of lexical entries is to find a representation which is sufficiently abstract to serve as input to different syntactic theories. By theories we do not only intend explicit grammatical frameworks, but also theories implicitly encoded in the program of a parser, generator, etc.

Although the descriptive goals are similar in most cases, differences can be found with respect to:

- the descriptive vocabulary used in different frameworks and the distinctions made;
- the amount of syntactic information that is encoded in the lexicon;
- the purpose which a certain application is to fulfil.

The central problem is to 'investigate in how far compromises or abstractions can be found that will provide at least fundamental syntactic information in the lexicon which can be augmented with theory specific information' (Rohrer, 1990). This problem is obviously directly connected with that of the re-usability of grammatical knowledge (see section 5.3.2).

The current situation of semantic theories constitutes an additional obstacle to the creation of standard semantic descriptions. Here, the very provisional and limited development of the various semantic approaches makes the comparison, the evaluation, and the abstraction process extremely difficult. In a certain sense, we are still at the stage of evaluating whether any approach has so far reached a sufficient degree of maturity for application to the semantic description of a large lexicon. A very promising approach, which, however, demands further research, seems to be that of lexical semantics, whose aim is also to interrelate regularities at the syntactical and semantic level. Lexical semantics (Pustejovsky, 1989) can be considered as an example of a theoretical development promoted by strict cooperation of linguists and computational linguists, in a certain sense similar to the LFG case mentioned above (section 4).[14]

The problem of including in the lexicon domain-specific world knowledge is certainly the most difficult. Only limited actions seem to be foreseeable in the immediate future such as, for example, to evaluate descriptive devices used in existing dictionaries in order to capture linguistic variation according to different pragmatic factors,

---

14. It seems that 'we have reached an interesting turning point in research, where linguistic studies can be informed by computational tools for lexicology as well as an appreciation of the computational complexity of large lexical databases' (Pustejovsky, 1989).

and to consider the role of these descriptions for preferential mechanisms in NL applications. Possibilities of standardizing the description of pragmatic stratification of the technical and scientific vocabulary in machine dictionaries for special purposes must be considered in connection with the inclusion of technology. (Rohrer, 1990).

Another interesting issue to be investigated in the near future is the feasibility of linking different monolingual dictionaries to yield a multilingual dictionary, possibly in the framework of a common underlying conceptual representation (Boguraev *et al.*, 1988).

3. Several types of partners must be involved, to contribute specific know-how and resources, and to represent various kinds of needs: linguists, computational linguists, humanists, industries, publishing houses. With the help of a carefully structured lexical database, it is possible to provide more coherent and informative dictionaries for human users. The consultation of both monolingual and bilingual electronic dictionaries for everyday use (CD-ROM, wordprocessors, etc.) can be greatly enhanced. For example, browsing techniques in a well-structured lexical database allow better access to any point of the dictionary. Appropriately structured dictionary definitions can be semi-automatically processed to generate a thesaurus of the general language. Links between monolingual and bilingual dictionaries allow searches for translation equivalents using families of conceptually interrelated words.[15]

5.3.2 Re-usability of grammatical knowledge: the polytheoretical issue
Most NLP systems are heavily based on grammatical components. Grammatical knowledge is represented in a formal language, which is usually very system-specific. As a consequence, the linguistic knowledge put into a component is not re-usable in other systems. Even the

---

15. Through appropriate semantic procedures, several types of semantic information implicitly embedded in the traditional lexicographical definitions can be extracted from machine-readable dictionaries and structured in a Lexical Knowledge Base (LKB). In this way, a specific word can be connected to other words through a network of various semantic-conceptual relations: synonymic, antinomic, taxonomic, etc. An LKB can be associated to a textual database (TDB), to increase the retrieval capabilities of the TDB user. Usually, the user of a TDB can search in the texts the occurrences (or co-occurrences) of word forms explicitly specified on the keyboard. If an LKB is available, the system can search not only the word form specified by the user, but also all the word forms connected to it in the LKB, both through morphological (inflectional variants) and conceptual-semantic links.

same project cannot easily modify or replace the formal representation language, without the risk of losing the results of an often huge bulk of work. A new project, adopting a different formalism, cannot re-use the grammatical knowledge embodied in another project, and the grammar rule writers must start from scratch. As a side effect, corpora annotated according to a given formalism cannot be easily exploited by other researchers. Following the example of very recent efforts in the field of lexical knowledge bases, the problem of the re-usability of grammatical knowledge is about to be faced.

One approach is to construct a grammatical knowledge representation that in some sense is more abstract than the system-specific representation, and can act as a 'neutral' basis from which various system-specific representations can be derived. The derivation will be fully automatic in the ideal case, but even if it were only interactive, this would already be a great improvement. The knowledge represented would not be entirely lost when a project would replace its system-specific grammar formalism; and there would be one formalism which could be shared, by linguists working in different environments, to communicate about descriptive questions (H. van Riemsdijk and L. des Tombe, 1990, personal communication).

Much intellectual effort will certainly be necessary to:

- compare in detail the various formalisms and grammatical theories;

- define and test a language for the abstract grammatical knowledge representation;

- define the interfaces necessary to semi-automatically generate grammars for some specific applications.

The theoretical relevance and implication of a polytheoretical approach to the description of linguistic knowledge at various levels is very controversial. Some linguists consider the goal of a 'polytheoretical' description unfeasible. Others consider it irrelevant if not counterproductive. Essentially linguistic theories should rely on explicative power. The description of real large subsets of natural languages is considered as a secondary task. On the contrary, other linguists assign, beside a practical value, also a theoretical interest to the polytheoretical approach.

A large, progressively incrementable, structured and formally explicit collection of information for different languages, not committed to a specific theory, is considered essential for the progress of research both at the monolingual and comparative level, as a source of data to be accounted for by the theories, and as a testbed for their evaluation. Some linguists also believe that the effort will show that most of the differences between linguistic theories could be considered as 'dialectal-social variations', which could be reduced and neutralized in order to allow the linguists to deal with more substantial problems. Ongoing projects (e.g. the Dutch project EUROGRAMMAR, and the ESF 'LANGUAGE TYPOLOGY'), aimed at compiling large encyclopedias on (comparative) grammars of various languages, will find these grammatical knowledge repositories a very useful tool, through which the data can be conveniently stored and accessed.

5.3.3 Textual reference corpora

Carefully constructed, large, written and spoken corpora are essential knowledge sources for:

1. Extensive description of the concrete use of language in real texts.

2. Identification of particular properties of linguistic units (various meanings, collocations, etc: cf. lexicographic practice).

3. Identification and characterization of sublanguages.

4. Studying frequencies and deriving probabilities.

National (British National Corpus, UK) and international (DCI, USA; NERC, Europe) corpora are being promoted. Humanists have a rich tradition, and precious data collections and know-how on corpus collection and processing.

It is necessary for linguistics, CL, AI, humanities, industries, publishing houses, to cooperate in developing:

- Methods to design the composition of corpora
- Standards for text representation and analysis annotation (cf the Text Encoding Initiative)[16]
- Tools for (semi)automatic linguistic analysis of large corpora

---

16. The Text Encoding Initiative, sponsored by the Association for Computers and the Humanities, the Association for Computational Linguistics and the Association for Computational Linguistics is preparing guidelines for the encoding of and the interchange of machine-readable texts using the Standard Generalized Markup Language.

- Methods for identification and characterization of sublanguages
- Adequate statistical models
- Methods for knowledge extraction from corpora
- Methods for collection and handling of spoken corpora
- Tools to reuse existing lexicographic, literary, and humanistic corpora
- Guidelines for dealing with (text) copyright problems

6 Concluding remarks: CL and other humanistic disciplines

Methods which have been developed in CL are not yet very commonly used in humanistic disciplines which use computers for text processing. There are many areas where CL methodology could be applied more, and a need for convergence is emerging between areas which, for various reasons, had very little contact in the past.

As examples of the consequence of the lack of communication, consider:

1. The know-how developed by humanistic disciplines in text collection, text representation, corpus linguistics, quantitative linguistics, text processing, style and sublanguages, lexicographic analysis, has been practically ignored by CL.

2. The majority of humanistic computing applications, frequency counts, concordance production, interactive text browsing, pattern recognition, information retrieval, etc., usually operate only on graphical (strings of textual characters), not on linguistic or conceptual units.

Researchers in the various lines must recognize that there is a need to exchange data and know-how, and cooperate to develop:

- Large reusable linguistic knowledge repositories (textual corpora, lexical databases, grammars)
- Robust taggers and analyzers
- Standards for linguistic data
- Specialized workstations, including intelligent browsing tools, for access to texts and dictionaries

- Computer-assisted procedures for expanding and integrating, through the interaction with reference sources, the linguistic and factual knowledge of the researcher interrogating the text.

They can find partners, resources, and support from the so-called language industries field. Multilingualism is a central aspect of language industries. The conservation of natural languages is an important factor for the preservation of national cultural identities. 'Informatization' has been indicated as a key element for the conservation of the vehicular function of a language. B. Quemada (1990, personal communication) has drawn an analogy between the introduction of printing and the informatization of languages. Languages which have not been involved with printing, have become dialects or have disappeared. The same thing could happen to languages that will not be 'informatized'.

References

Allen, J. (1987) **Natural Language Understanding,** (i) p. 2. Menlo Park, California: Benjamin Cumming.

ALPAC (1966) National Research Council. Automatic Language Processing Advisory Committee. **Language and Machine-Computers in Translation and Linguistics.** Washington, DC: National Academy of Sciences, National Research Council.

Bindi, R. and Calzolari, N. (1990) Statistical analysis of a large textual Italian corpus in search of lexical information. In **Proceedings of the EURALEX 1990 Conference** (Malaga).

Bobrow, D.G. and Winograd, T. (1977) An overview of KRL: a knowledge representation language. **Cognitive Science,** 1, 3-46.

Boguraev, B., Briscoe, T., Calzolari, N., Cater, A., Meijs, W., and Zampolli, A. (1988) **Acquisition of Lexical Knowledge for Natural Language Processing Systems (ACQUILEX).** Technical Annex, ESPRIT Basic Research Action No. 3030. Unpublished.

Bozzi, A. and Cappelli, G. (1987) The Latin lexical database and problems of standardization in the analysis of Latin texts. In **Data Networks for the Historical Disciplines,** edited by F. Hausmann, pp. 28-45. Graz: Leykam-Verlag.

Bresnan, J. (1982) Editor. **The Mental Representation of Grammatical Relations.** Cambridge, Mass.: MIT Press.

Bruce, B. (1975) Case Systems for Natural Language. **Artificial Intelligence**, 6, 327-360.

Calzolari, N. (1988) The dictionary and the thesaurus can be combined. In **Relational Models of the Lexicon**, edited by M. Evans, pp. 75-96. Cambridge: Cambridge University Press.

Calzolari, N. and Picchi, E. (1988) Acquisition of semantic information from an on-line dictionary. In **Proceedings of the 12th COLING** (Budapest, 1988), pp.87-92.

Calzolari, N. and Zampolli, A. (1991) Lexical databases and textual corpora: a trend of convergence between computational linguistics and literary and linguistic computing. In **Research in Humanities Computing**, edited by S. Hockey and N. Ide, pp. 273- 307. Oxford: Oxford University Press.

Colmerauer, A. (1978) Metamorphosis Grammar. Natural Language Communication with Computers. In **Lecture Notes in Computer Science**, vol.63, edited by Leonard Bolc. Berlin: Springer.

Dresher, B.E. and Hornstein, N. (1976) On some supposed contributions of artificial intelligence to the scientific study of language. **Cognition**, 4, 321-398.

Dresher, B.E. and Hornstein, N. (1977a) Response to Schank and Vilensky. **Cognition**, 5, 147-150.

Dresher, B.E. and Hornstein, N. (1977b) Reply to Winograd. **Cognition**, 5, 377-392.

Fillmore, C. (1968) A case for Case. In **Universals in Linguistic Theory**, edited by E. Bach and R.T. Harms. New York: Rinehart Winston.

Fillmore, C. (1977) Scenes-and-frames semantics. In **Linguistic Structures Processing**, edited by A. Zampolli, pp.55-82. Amsterdam: North-Holland.

Friedman, J. (1971) **A Computer Model of Transformational Grammar**. New York: Elsevier.

Garside, R., Leech, G. and Sampson, G. (1987) Editors. **The Computational Analysis of English**. London and New York: Longman.

Gazdar, G., Klein, E., Pullum, G.K., and Sag, I.A. (1985) **Generalized Phrase Structure Grammar**. Cambridge, Mass.: Harvard University Press.

Grishmann, R. (1986) **Computational Linguistics,** (i) p.146. Cambridge: Cambridge University Press.

Halliday, M. (1990) Invited lecture at the 1990 AILA World Congress, Thessaloniki (not yet published).

Kaplan, R. (1973) A general syntactic processor. In **Natural Language Processing,** edited by R. Rustin, pp. 193-241. New York: Algorithmics Press.

Karlgren, H. (1973) Foreword. In **Computational and Mathematical Linguistics,** edited by A.Zampolli and N. Calzolari, pp. xiii-xiv. Firenzi: Olschki.

Kay, M. (1973) The MIND system. In **Natural Language Processing,** edited by R. Rustin, pp. 155-188. New York: Algorithmics Press.

Kay, M. (1982) Grammatico-semantic analysis. **The Prague Bulletin of Mathematical Linguistics,** 39, 110-113.

Kay, M. (1985) Parsing in Functional Unification Grammar. In **Natural Language Parsing,** edited by D.R. Dowty, L. Karttunen and A. Zwicky, pp.251-278. New York: Cambridge University Press.

Koskenniemi, K. (1983) **Two-Level Morphology: a general computational model for word-form recognition and production,** University of Helsinki, Dept. of General Linguistics, Publication no.11, Helsinki.

Kuhn, T. (1970) **The Structure of Scientific Revolution,** 2nd edn. Chicago: University of Chicago Press.

McCord, M. (1980) Slot Grammars. **American Journal of Computational Linguistics,** 6, 1, 31-43.

Minsky, M. (1975) A Framework for Representing Knowledge. In **Psychology of Computer Vision,** edited by P.H. Winston. McGraw-Hill.

Nagao, M. (1989) **Machine Translation—How Far Can It Go?** Oxford: Oxford University Press.

Perschke, S. (1988) **Hearing on the language industry in the European community. Questions put to the participants.** (Background paper for discussion).

Picchi, E. (1988) **D.B.T. A Full-Text Data Base System: Methods and Tools for Searching Full-Text Data.** Pisa:ILC. Internal report.

Pollard, C., and Sag, I.A. (1987) **Information-based Syntax and Semantics**, Vol.I. Stanford: CLSI.

Pustejovsky, J. (1989) Current issues in computational semantics. In **Proceedings of the 4th Conference of the European Chapter of the ACL** (Manchester, 1989) pp. xvii-xxv.

Rohrer, C. (1990) **EUROTRA-7, Feasibility and Project Definition Study on the Reusability of Lexical and Terminological Resources in Computerized Applications**. Presented to the EEC. Unpublished.

Schank, R. (1975) **Conceptual Information Processing**, Amsterdam: North-Holland.

Schank, R. and Abelson, R. (1977) **Scripts, Plans, Goals and Understanding**. Hillsdale, NJ: Erlbaum.

Schmolze, J.G. and Brachmann, R.J. (1982) **Proceedings of the 1981 KL-ONE Workshop**, Fairchild Technical Report no. 618.

Smith, J. (1973) Ideals versus practicalities in linguistic data processing. In **Computational and Mathematical Linguistics**, edited by A.Zampolli and N. Calzolari, pp. 895-898. Firenzi: Olschki.

Wilensky, R., (1981) PAM and MICRO-PAM. In **Inside Computer Understanding**, edited by R. Schank and C. Riesbeck, pp.136-96. Hillsdale, New Jersey: Laurence Erlbaum Associates.

Wilks, Y. (1975) An Intelligent Analyzer and Understander of English. **Comm. ACM**, 18, 5, 264-74.

Winograd, T. (1977) On some contested suppositions of generative linguistics about the scientific study of language. **Cognition**, 5, 151-179.

Winograd, T. (1983) **Language as a Cognitive Process**. Syntax, (i) p.20. Reading, Massachusetts: Addison-Wesley.

Woods, W. (1970) Transition network grammars for natural language analysis. **CAMC** 13:10, 591-606.

Woods, W. (1975) What's in a Link: Foundations for semantic networks. In **Representation and Understanding**, edited by D.Bobrow and A. Collins. New York: Academic Press.

Zampolli, A. (1973) Introduction. In **Computational and Mathematical Linguistics**, edited by A.Zampolli and N. Calzolari, pp. xix-xxviii. Firenzi: Olschki.

Zampolli, A. (1975) **Problemi di linguistica applicata computazionale**. Pisa: CNUCE-CNR.

Zampolli, A. and Calzolari, N. (1973) Editors. **Computational and Mathematical Linguistics**. Firenzi: Olschki.

Zampolli, A. and Hockey, S. (1990). Unpublished Memorandum on Computing in the Humanities, presented to the European Science Foundation.

Scholarship and Technology in Classical Studies

W.R. Connor

National Humanities Center, North Carolina

Over the past few decades classical studies have acquired a remarkable new wardrobe. Classicists can now clad themselves in a comprehensive, accessible, and relatively inexpensive panoply for the computerized study of the subject matter of the field. It could be argued that no other humanistic field (except perhaps linguistics) has comparable access to such comprehensive and sophisticated computerization. '"Ten years ahead of the rest of us", is a common comment about how much farther along classics scholars are in their use of computers than are those in other humanities disciplines', asserts the *Chronicle of Higher Education* (July 12, 1989).

Such comments provoke a twinge in this classicist. They make me think *back* a decade or so, rather than forward to the happy day when the rest of the humanities will be equally well dressed. That reaction may be in part the nostalgia of a lapsed McLuhanite, one who believed that the new technology would open up a new range of questions about the ancient world, provide fresh strategies for approaching both these problems and some grand but intractable questions inherited from the past. I confess I had hoped that computer technology would help classicists take on intellectually more ambitious questions and answer them in fresh ways. It has contributed to the intellectual invigoration of the field, in my view, but far less than I would have expected or hoped.

My sense of disappointment is heightened by a recent development in classical studies: the recognition of the effects of literacy on Greek society. Scholarship has emphasized how far reaching were the effects of the Greek adoption (and modification) of the semitic alphabet. What began as a convenience turned out, if recent analyses are correct, to have far reaching effects on how people lived and thought. Our awareness of the consequences of this change in technology increases the expectation that computer-based technology might in our society have analogous effects and result in significant changes in the way in which scholars conceptualize their material. If this has not as yet happened in any fundamental sense, we should bear in mind that the changes in the Greek world went on for centuries. *Sed adhuc tua messis in herba est.*

But let us begin with a quick tour of the classicist's stylish new wardrobe and then ask what American classicists are doing with their finery. On that basis we can advance some suggestions and speculations about scholarly developments in this field in the next decade.

Description of the resources

The development of computer applications in classical studies owes a great deal to two individuals, Theodore Brunner of the Thesaurus Linguae Graecae and David Packard, the developer of the IBYCUS and the founder of the Packard Humanities Institute. Thanks to them and their allies—private donors, private foundations such as the Packard Foundation, governmental sources, notably the National Endowment for the Humanities, and the University of California and others—all Greek literature is now available in machine readable form down to approximately 632 AD. This totals approximately 62,000,000 words. Data entry is continuing among Byzantine texts. The costs to the user are modest, and the quality is very high.

Other efforts, particularly those at the Packard Humanities Institute in Los Altos California, have made a large portion of Latin literature available in comparable form. Stephen Waite reports that most Latin texts written before 200 AD are now available and that the entry of fragments, Servius' commentary on Vergil and Justinian's law code are progressing steadily. In addition certain post-medieval Greek texts have been entered. Projects are under way, moreover, to make other kinds of classical texts and data accessible in machine readable form. A project at Duke University, under the leadership of William Willis, John Oates, and others, has succeeded in entering substantial numbers of documentary papyri. Epigraphical texts are being entered in several centres in North America and are conveniently described in the *Actes du colloque 'Epigraphie et informatique'* published by the Institut d'archéologie et d'histoire ancienne of the University of Lausanne.

This material can be utilized in several ways. The printing of indices or lengthy lists has almost entirely given way in North America to interactive computing. Large machines, typically in university computation centres, are now much less commonly used than personal computers. The availability of all the TLG material on a single CD-ROM makes it highly convenient for the personal computer. The absence of convenient software for consulting this material through IBM systems is perhaps the single greatest impediment to its full utilization. But many classicists have found Apple computers can be readily adapted to this material. More impressive, however, is the second generation of David Packard's IBYCUS machine. This machine combines easy access to the TLG material and other texts, a wide variety of fonts for non-Roman alphabets and powerful wordprocessing capacity. When I visit classics departments at the major universities throughout the country, I find that they almost all have access to an IBYCUS or an Apple machine suitable for the TLG material. Many of the smaller colleges, an often neglected but very important part of classical studies in the United States, and many individual classicists have also purchased one of these systems or a modem that allows access to the machine readable texts.

Any list of computer based projects in classical studies on the North American continent is likely to be incomplete, since new projects emerge with considerable frequency. But no survey should fail to mention the efforts to utilize the computer for improved bibliographies in the classical field. In cooperation with the central office of the project in Paris, the computer is now being used more extensively for the annual entry of data for the volumes of *L'année philologique*, the principal bibliographical resource in classical studies. The American office, in Chapel Hill, North Carolina, has vigorously supported the use of the computer for such work. A project is also underway to make past volumes of *L'année philologique* available in computerized form. Optical scanner technology holds out the promise that this project can be carried out at a reasonable cost.

Pedagogical applications are also appearing—in very varied forms. This is not the place to survey pedagogical uses, but one, the Perseus Project, centred at Harvard University, and supported largely by the Annenberg Foundation, is of special interest. Under the day to day guidance of Gregory Crane, Greek texts, translations, maps, Landsat, and other cartographic material, photographs of sites, architecture, and vase paintings are being compiled in such a way that they can be utilized through the hypercard feature on Apple and comparable machines. It will be readily apparent to anyone who works with the Perseus system that it has important implications for research as well as for teaching.

These developments have not been centrally planned or directed. They have, however, received the encouragement of various classical organizations, especially the American Philological Association. The work of individuals, committees, and boards need not be surveyed here, although the work of Dee Clayman deserves special mention. She has consistently, quietly, and effectively advanced the cause of computerized studies of the classics. The support of the major classical associations in the United States reflects a solid base of support among individual classicists. To be sure there have been sceptics and even luddites among American classicists, but in general the developments described here have been received with enthusiasm. The most common complaint is that more has not been done sooner.

The enthusiasm is based, no doubt, on the wide recognition that computerized access to texts is especially important in fields such as classical studies that lack access to native speakers. The interpretation of word, phrase, and idiom, the determination of semantic range, connotation, nuance, and so forth, which in a modern spoken language might be done by consulting a few native speakers, requires access to large numbers of texts. Thus for the most basic philological reasons computerized access to texts has a strong appeal to the traditional core of classical studies.

Thus far an American success story—innovative, fast paced, and (relatively) well funded technological change; a model cooperation among private donors, foundations, federal government, and universities; a door opened to a new way of practising the most traditional of the humanities.

Applications

And so we behold before us the new model American classicist—clad in the breastplate of a CPU, girt with cables and perhaps even fibre optics, with CD-ROM upon his shield, floppy disks in his right hand and monitor on his left. O tempora, o modems!

But having put on the full armour of the computer, what battles does this warrior now fight? Here the story becomes more difficult to trace. The effects of computer technology are often hard to discern and the observations that follow are impressionistic rather than systematic. Let us begin with the least difficult and problematic applications and move toward the more difficult issues.

Wordprocessing

Here the computer has clearly triumphed, relegating the yellow pad and the typewriter to the same museum as the stylus and the papyrus. To be sure, it is impossible to tell whether an individual published article was prepared on a typewriter or a wordprocessor, but there is no doubt what has happened. The convenience of using the computer for scholarly writing swiftly became evident, even when machines were ill adapted to produce Greek and other non-Roman fonts. As costs have gone down, and new software programs have been developed, the attractions have increased. The newer machines, especially the Apples and the IBYCUS, conquer the remaining typographic problems and greatly simplify the tasks of scholarly writing. The new generation of scholars now entering the profession, accustomed to computers in their school years, now expect a wordprocessor in their studies, much as they expect desks and bookshelves.

Bibliographic management

It is but a small step from wordprocessing to bibliographical management. A certain amount can be done with the search capacity on most wordprocessing programs, and other more sophisticated programs are easy to acquire and use. The extent of their use is, however, once again hard to determine, but there is every reason to expect that it is substantial and growing. As major bibliographical reference works, such as *L'année philologique*, become available on CD-ROM, as other databases are developed, and as scholars become accustomed to consulting libraries through electronic catalogues, we can expect that scholars will develop more sophisticated forms of individual bibliographical management.

Other forms of data management

Archaeology provides perhaps the best example of the advantages of computer technology for data management in classical studies. Excavators, and museum curators are making extensive use of computers and no doubt will continue to do so.

Publication

It has now become common for university presses and many scholarly journals to ask that final copy for publication be submitted both on diskette and on a printout. The advantages to the publisher are obvious and the problems, notably the diversity of formats, presumably will diminish, if, as is often predicted, there is a reduction in the number of wordprocessing programs on the market. One would expect increasing speed and reduced costs for scholarly publication as a result of the new technologies.

Text consultation

It is again difficult to determine the extent of use of the new technologies. While those who use the TLG material are obligated to acknowledge the fact in their published work, there is no way to determine the extent to which they heed this injunction. One cannot tell whether an individual text cited in a scholarly article or book was consulted in printed form or on the monitor's screen, unless the author chooses to provide an acknowledgement. As will appear below, there are relatively few such acknowledgements in recent publications in the classical field, but we must be careful lest we attach excessive significance to this *argumentum ex silentio*. The convenience of consulting texts, especially the obscurer ones, on CD-ROM rather than through a visit to the library provides a strong incentive for the adoption of the new technology. There is, however, one obstacle, the lack of a convenient way to consult textual variants and conjectures.

This list of the effects of computer technology on classical studies could no doubt be expanded, and the extent of current use be determined with much greater precision. The overall picture, however, is clear enough, or so it seems. The new technology is widely available, relatively inexpensive and there are strong incentives for its adoption. In time the standard operating procedure for a classicist will be to call up texts on the screen of his or her computer, split the screen or switch screens to consult bibliographical databases, use ever more convenient wordprocessing programs to write up the results of the investigations, and submit the finished material to a publisher on a diskette or similar form. Even if we leave aside such questions as whether electronic 'publication' will replace more traditional forms of scholarly communication, we should feel some confidence in predicting greater speed and convenience of research at every stage.

These predictions of a rosy future, however, find only partial confirmation in the present. Although wordprocessing has become standard and the use of other computer applications is growing, the results are rather less than dramatic. Perhaps we can all express relief that the amount of scholarly publication at least as judged by the number of articles submitted to major journals, is not increasing. But speed does not seem to be increasing either. Would anyone argue that scholarly publication in the field is appearing more promptly? Some might contend that while the pace remains glacial, the new technology has helped contain the *costs* of publication. I would welcome evidence on this point, especially if it could be shown that such savings as have emerged are not simply the result of shifting routine editorial tasks from press employees onto authors. This practice seems to me a waste of intellectual capital.

And what shall we say about the *quality* of classical scholarship? Has it improved thanks to the computer? I believe it has, but only in modest ways. The search capacities of the IBYCUS and comparable systems allow a much higher degree of accuracy and comprehensiveness than is possible through consultation of printed lexica and indices. One can point to some important studies in stylistics and metrics that have been made possible by computer technology. Papyrologists have succeeded in identifying and placing fragments that might otherwise have remained in their storage boxes. The list could be expanded, and no doubt will be as new texts are entered and new projects completed.

These examples need to be measured, however, against the base line of articles and monographs which show no signs of having utilized the new technology. If one surveys recent issues of the principal North American and British journals containing studies of classical Greek literature and history, for example, one will find very few acknowledgments of the TLG material and very few signs that the new computer technology has been used for anything other than wordprocessing and routine bibliographical management. The newly arrived volume 119 of the *Transactions of the American Philological Association* is typical,— and significant because it is a journal that carries a relatively large percentage of articles by younger American classicists. These are precisely the scholars who might be expected to make use of the new computer technologies. Yet among the twenty four articles in the volume I find only one, an investigation of the word *orthros*, that shows signs of a serious use of the computer.

A similar impression emerges from most monographs in the field that I have recently seen. Those that use the new technology in anything more than a routine way are few and far between.

This fact may be discounted in various ways: perhaps it is too early for the technology to have penetrated a staid and traditional discipline. Yet classicists have clearly acclaimed and welcomed the new technology.

Perhaps those who are computer minded have directed their energies to data entry and program development and have little energy left over for scholarly problems. Yet given the power of the computer colleagues less versed in its operation might be expected to turn to these skilled practitioners for help in working on the problems that concern them most directly. Or perhaps classicists are so careless or lacking in gratitude that they use the technology without acknowledging the fact. Yet the articles and monographs themselves do not show signs of any extensive use of the new techniques.

The emperor's closet

One is driven then to ask the unpleasant question: Does the emperor have new clothes but prefers not to wear them? Is the classical profession, for all the admiration directed to its splendid new attire, content to go about clad in what God and nineteenth century philology granted it? If the answer to these questions is a qualified 'Yes', as I rather think it is, then we might speculate 'Why?' and whether the emperor will eventually reach into his closet and make use of his new attire.

My suspicion is that the computer technology became available precisely at the wrong moment in the profession's development. The era of traditional lexical and textual studies had largely passed, except in those specialities where the computer was slowest to penetrate—papyrology and epigraphy and the texts of late antiquity and the byzantine period. Word indices and concordances in printed form had become more accessible thanks to new publication and the reprinting of out of print volumes. Textually minded scholars found the absence of an apparatus criticus in the computerized material reduced its utility. They naturally stayed with printed texts or facsimiles. The past decade has not produced a large number of American studies devoted to stylistics, chronological sequence or authorship questions—areas in which the computer might be expected to make major contributions. Something similar might be said of commentaries: while the computer can be very valuable in preparing a commentary, American classical scholarship in recent years has left this estimable activity largely to colleagues across the water.

The energy of North American classicists, by and large, has concentrated on interpretive questions and on the writing of essays and monographs of social themes, cultural history, and literary criticism. Here too the computer might prove useful, but the particular form of recent

American classical scholarship made its application more difficult. Literary criticism, for example, turned away from the emphasis on the recurrence of motif, image, and phrase so central in the New Criticism and concentrated on structural patterns, links with myth and ritual, the way in which social roles were depicted and on related theoretical concerns. Or consider the fate of the allusion. Not so many years ago the recognition of a hitherto undetected allusion could be a source of some distinction for a classicist. Today there would be little to be gained from noting an allusion unless it could be shown to contribute to the understanding of the intertextuality of the work. The questions posed by Feminist, Marxist, Structuralist, and Post-Structuralist criticism have not lent themselves to computer-based responses. Even Homeric studies, where the systematic analysis of the formula invites the use of computer technology, was in a period of 'soft Parryism' in which other approaches dominated.

In historical studies too the times were out of joint. The great era of prosopographical analyses of political events had passed. In intellectual history the computer might be expected to have been of great use. But again the timing seems to have been wrong. The sophisticated searching capacities of the computer were well suited to word studies but less well adapted to what might be called 'the imported concept'—analytical categories not present in the Greek language itself but very useful for the understanding of Greek society and attitudes. Thus the computer might readily be applied to *dike*, *hybris*, or *pleonexia*—topics well studied in earlier scholarship—but required more sophistication to deal with concepts of 'sovereignty', 'citizenship', 'imperialism', 'ideology' or 'neutrality'—let alone 'embodiment' (See J. Ober *Classical Philology* 84, 4 (1989) p. 324) or 'state'. None of these terms coincides precisely with an ancient Greek term. Rather they are modern concepts applied to an ancient civilization. Although some classicists object to the apparent anachronism involved, I am convinced that the use of such concepts is legitimate, but requires care and sophistication.

A discussion that has been quite central in recent treatments of Athenian democracy provides a useful example. There has been lively discussion of late of the tension between 'popular sovereignty' and 'the rule of law' in classical Athenian civic life. Historians have asked whether we can see a transition from one to the other, and whether the two should be viewed as antitheses. Although the discussion has been useful, the formulation does not coincide precisely with ancient terminology. As best I can tell the computer has not been used extensively in the research behind these discussions.

A case could be made, I believe, that the discussion would benefit from a more rigorous analysis of the relationship between these 'imported' concepts and some ancient analogues. To do so, however, would require an extensive study of the semantic field for political values in classical Attic Greek. For that the computer would be of the greatest value. To be sure it would need to be used with great care and sophistication and supplemented with studies of civic institutions, rituals, and other practices. The results, however, might be very welcome at this moment in Greek historical studies.

Such projects await skilled and ambitious scholars. At this moment, however, the trends in scholarship point in the other direction and help us understand the limited use of computer technology in classical studies. It is not surprising that some critics regard the computer as at best a convenient way of doing wordprocessing, but, in so far as scholarship is concerned, a toy or stylish new garment, enjoyable for a while but likely in time to be relegated to the closet. Such critics see data entry, the development of databanks and programs as distractions of the energy available for serious scholarship.

Such criticism has some force at the present time, but what of the next generation? Those who are now entering the profession were trained in computers in the grade schools, lived with them on their desks in college, have friends and roommates who know the technology enough to be making their living designing or selling such machines and software. Surely we have every reason to expect more innovative and imaginative applications as a new generation, fully trained in computers, enters the profession.

Or so the unregenerate McLuhanite hopes. The technology of literacy took generations to work through the Greek world and reshape it. Computer technology will also take time to realize its full potential. Perhaps there is then reason to hope that the new generation will learn to formulate new questions and indeed to think through computers in a way that those of us in an earlier generation are unlikely to do.

Many of these questions may turn out to be of such complexity that several scholars will need to be involved in answering them. Humanistic scholarship in general, and classical scholarship especially, has remained a cottage industry while scientific research and that in the social sciences has become ever more collaborative. There is much, I believe, that only the individual scholar can do, but many of the most challenging questions in the field are simply too big for one person. If so, the most important developments in technology may be in the improved ability to exchange information and ideas quickly and conveniently. The impediment to collaborative research is only partly geographical separation. The gravest difficulty is the glacial pace of communication in humanistic fields, the assumption that only published material needs to be taken seriously and the tolerance of delays of years from the formulation of an idea to its ultimate dissemination.

In the last few years we have seen the emergence of electronic mail, fax systems, and the increasing prominence of the conference as a means of scholarly exchange. These are important antidotes to the poisonous effects that the delays in publication impose on the development of new ideas. This technology may ultimately prove of even greater importance than the computer itself in changing and invigorating classical scholarship. Perhaps the emperor will feel happier in this suit of clothes.

History, Historians and the New Technology

Deian Hopkin, University College of Wales, and

Peter Denley, University of London

Frequent reports of the death of history are greatly exaggerated. Yet concern about its state of health has been a recurring discussion point for some considerable time. In a study of historiography published in 1984, John Tosh concluded that the bleak and uncertain outlook for history in the 1960s had given way to 'the invigorating effects of ... a surge of innovations', by which he meant the collective impact of developments such as the use of theory, quantitative analysis or oral history, and the adoption of interpretative frameworks of cultural anthropology or human geography (Tosh, 1984). Others have been less sanguine. Lawrence Stone (1987i) believed that a heroic age of historiography had come to an end, while David Cannadine, in a memorable survey of British historiography published in *Past and Present* in 1987, described a state of 'gloom, despondency and alarm' (Cannadine, 1987i). This drew the response from one critic that his diagnosis was 'partial and questionable, the perspective distorted and the implied cure dangerous as well as inapplicable' (Cross, Lamont and Evans, 1988). A friendly lot, historians.

Whatever the diagnosis, the symptoms are clear enough. In a recent compilation entitled *What is History Today*, a group of some seventy historians were canvassed for short statements about their view of current historical thinking and research. The answers were distributed among thirteen separate sections, dealing with everything from politics to women, from the military to the mind (Gardiner, 1988). Even then, it is clear that further subdivisions might have been generated. The only section that was missing was the eponymous one: What is history? Clearly the answer to the whole question lay in the sum of the subsidiary answers.

Of course, this is an old story. One of the most widely used student texts in historiography, prepared over thirty years ago, offered twenty-seven varieties of historical writing including 'the New History' (Stern,

1956). And the very phrase, The New History, has been used from time to time to indicate seminal shifts in perception or preoccupation and to offer hope for future development (Rabb and Rotberg, 1982). Yet historians have been increasingly concerned with the contraction in the general field of history through the expansion of the specialisms (Fieldhouse, 1983-84; Bender, 1985).

There has, of course, been expansion of another, more physical, kind. Perhaps the most striking feature of History in the past thirty years has been the sheer production of historians. Even if the rate of growth has been reduced to a mere trickle, the bulk of this historical profession is still with us, slowly passing through into middle and early old age. With so much emphasis nowadays on published output as a measure of performance, it is hardly surprising that one growth industry is journal abstraction. A recent publication devoted to a review of periodical material on British History published in 1988 cited 140 different journals in which relevant articles appeared (*International Review of Periodical Literature*, 1989). Since then there have been numerous additions to the list. Monographs, text books, Festschriften, essays—that is yet another dimension of bibliographic horror. In 1989, the *British National Bibliography* listed 60,000 items published in English, of which some 10 per cent were related to history. One can sympathize with the editor of a new journal who regretted:

> The study of history in our times is becoming increasingly important, and it is more and more difficult, even for the professional scholar, to keep up to date with all the discoveries and with all the new research which is being produced every day in this vast field.

But that was Gabriel Monod, the journal was the *Revue historique*, and the year was 1876.

An attempt to encompass historical writing in a paper such as this cannot succeed, yet it is possible to offer some general points for discussion through examining selected developments, largely confined to Europe, which offer pointers to wider concerns.

The reorientation of the subject

The new varieties of history are a reflection of the increasing diversity of life itself; the more complex social activity becomes, the more complex its history. Moreover, if we are to accept the claims of Sir

Geoffrey Elton (1969i) that 'historical study is not the study of the past but the study of present traces of the past' it follows that the task of the historian becomes infinitely more difficult in a society which is obsessed with documenting its own activities. In this respect the modern historian envies the medievalist the relative containment and stability of his source material, which in turn enables the scholar to engage in the close study of a defined and limited range of texts. This is an enterprise in which few historians of modern politics or society can afford to indulge. The penalty, however, is a more impressionistic account of modern history than should be the case, with the historian forced to select material from a vast range.

For this reason it is perhaps no accident that many of the most important advances in historiography have come from historians of the medieval or early modern periods. It is they who have succeeded in integrating the techniques and accomplishments of other disciplines. It is always invidious to single out items of historical work, if only because inevitably one is confined to those areas with which one is most familiar. But few would dispute the claims to historiographical pre-eminence of Keith Thomas' *Religion and the Decline of Magic* (1971). One of Sir Keith's achievements, reinforced in his later volume, *Man and the Natural World* (1983), was to use the techniques of anthropologists, geographers and even biologists to weave his way through otherwise impenetrable source material. The Braudelian canvas, moreover, extending over centuries, has given such studies unusual perspectives. Few have succeeded in emulating this accomplishment but a number of historians have come to recognize, for example, that the study of formal institutions or ordered political behaviour in isolation reveals relatively little about life itself. The study of popular culture, by contrast, whether in Reformation Germany (Scribner, 1987) or in the sixteenth-century Netherlands (Schama, 1977, 1988) can transform our understanding of the interrelationship between highly localized belief and generalized political activity.

Nor need the canvas be as extensive or as ambitious. A genre which has made a considerable impact in recent years has been the micro-historical study, the elaborate study of an event. Emmanuel Le Roy Ladurie's *Carnival at Romans* (1981) or Robert Darnton's *The Great Cat Massacre* (1984) may be very small worlds turned upside down, but they have a universal focus.

The last few years have also witnessed a debate of some interest over the respective roles of narrative and analysis (Stone, 1987ii). In some respects, this is a vindication of the very idea that historians reflect their age, for as the structured theories of Marxism and positivism have become increasingly challenged and ideas of individualism and free will revived, so historians have become aware of the implications of this for their own subject. If Christopher Hill and Eric Hobsbawm were the products of an age which sought universal panaceas through social welfarism and collectivism, then John Vincent and Jonathan Clark reflect the increasing fascination with the contingent effect of high and individual politics (Cooke and Vincent, 1974; Clark, 1982). Yet this need not be merely traditional. Simon Schama's celebratory volume, *Citizens* (1989), published during the bicentennial of the French Revolution, is a narrative epic in the classic mould which nevertheless offers fresh insights into the lives of ordinary people, a concern usually associated with more recent historiography.

Just as the single event can become the paradigm for the longue durée, so the study of region or province can reveal as much as the study of central place or metropolis. One of the most admired books by a medievalist, which won the 1987 Wolfson Prize for History, is Professor Rees Davies' study of Welsh society and politics in the thirteenth and fourteenth centuries (1987). What all these books have in common is a powerful awareness of language, reflected in luminous and highly readable prose. Historians have, in any case, become more sensitive to the power of language in history. In this respect historiography has still much to learn from structuralism and deconstruction.

But it is not just a matter of artefacts and material. History is not observed from a static platform, situated in a permanent and unchanging anchorage, from which some enduring vision of the past can be recorded. The vantage point is itself continuously changing. As David Lowenthal recently observed in a recent and unusual historiographical survey (1985i),

> Without a past that is malleable as well as generously preserved, the present will lack models to inspire it, and the future will be deprived of a lifeline to its past ... By changing relics and records of former times, we change ourselves as well; the revised past in turn alters our own identity.

Computers and the changing world of the historian

Nothing is more likely to alter the capacity of both society to change its present and for historians to change the past than the advent of the computer. Of course, computing is in a long line of technological changes which have altered the perspectives of historians. The advent of paper and printing and the emergence of the mass media are two which have most directly affected the historian. It is important to emphasize, however, that by technology we must not mean current technology alone; nor should we confine our attention to the computer. Historians must be concerned with the widest impact of technology, and a significant number of them, notably in the United States, have indeed been interested in the role of film and other media, including the press, on historical processes. Others have been more directly concerned with the relationship between technology itself and history (notably the challenge to positivism). A more recent development has been an interest in the way technology can reinforce and even alter the way historians themselves work. But these things should not be confused. They are a mixture of ends and means.

Yet it is fair to say that the use of technology, and even the study of technology in the broad sense in which we have defined it, is still a marginal activity, judged in pure volume terms. Historians, in the main, only make passing reference to the press and to the media, and rarely study them systematically. Instead, the contents of newspapers are treated like any other source; and a more quotable source than newspaper editorials is difficult to find in modern history. The study of film or the media is still regarded as a fringe activity, however central such media may be to the 'real world'. To this extent, historians have yet to embrace the technological imperatives of their own contemporaries. Now all of this may be the product of that disjunction between the historical profession and the age itself. If historians have reflected change in their own age, it has usually been through the youngest of them. If there is a crisis in history, indeed, it may be a crisis of demography, not of the discipline.

On the face of it, historians have been slow to acknowledge and embrace computers. Whilst many subjects, as diverse as classical studies and geography, linguistics and music, have seen great activity in this field, historians have often been accused of being more reticent. It is true that the organization of historical computing has been relatively slow compared with, say, that of literary and linguistic studies. Yet it would be misleading to pursue this form of comparison. History is an enormous subject, touching most others, and in some fields computers have been widely used for many years, especially where quantitative methods were already being applied. Individual historians were using computers very early in the evolution of the technology—one thinks of the work of Wrigley and Schofield on British demography or Speck on eighteenth-century elections (Wrigley and Schofield, 1981; cf. also Speck and Gray, 1970; Speck, Gray and Hopkinson, 1975. For a general survey, Denley, 1984, 1990). Others were well aware of the potential even if they could not make direct use of the technology themselves (e.g. Thernstrom, 1973). Major computer-based projects have been under way for many years. It is the absence of an obvious central forum or common agenda which has perhaps inhibited the diffusion of such work.

In recent years, however, it would be no exaggeration to say that there has been a minor revolution in attitudes, fuelled by the advent of convenient and affordable wordprocessors and the simultaneous disappearance of departmental secretaries (certainly in support of most scholarship). Increasingly historians who have no direct use for computers as such have come to recognize their potential. At the very least, there are fewer sceptics than hitherto. The revolution, moreover, has begun to affect all aspects of the historian's work, from research and writing to teaching.

The most obvious advances have been made in research, not least in those subject areas where the material has been difficult to organize. The first two volumes of transactions of the Association of History and Computing provide an insight into the range and quality of this work and lays to rest, once and for all, the widely-held assumption that computers are only relevant to quantification (Denley and Hopkin, 1987; Denley, Harvey and Fogelvik, 1989; see also *Computer Applications in the Historical Sciences*, 1989-90; Mawdsley *et al.*, 1990). Inevitably, and properly, quantification plays an important part, and there is no doubt that the advent of the computer has stimulated work on statistical analysis and modelling (for an overview, see Jarausch, Arminger and Thaller, 1985). It has also made such techniques available to a wider band of historians who find the prepared package a convenient and accessible tool. The historian who deals with individuals and communities has also benefited. The processes of nominal record linkage, family and community reconstitution and prosopography, are all expedited by computers (e.g. Millet, 1985). In many cases they are only possible through machine-based processing because of the size and distribution of the data, the complexities of the linkages and the intricacies of the algorithms. How many historians in the past could ever have contemplated projects on the scale of the SOREP demographic study of Quebec, which uses a database of half a million French inhabitants (Pouyez *et al.*, 1983; *Reconstitution automatique des familles*, 1988), or the PortBooks project at Wolverhampton which explores the implications for the economy of early industrial England of 50,000 voyages and cargoes (Wakelin, 1987)? The combination of text analysis and statistics offers the prospect of using source material in an entirely new way; the DEEDS of Essex project at Toronto uses the Feet of Fines and the charters contained in the Hospitaller Cartularies, over a period of two centuries, to examine topics as varied as the incidence and distribution of occupations, the nature of land-holding and the evolution of legal terminology (Gervers, 1987).

At the same time, historians are becoming aware of their own particular software requirements. In the past, there were two choices; either to accept, warts and all, the widely available and well-supported but often inadequate business applications software, or to learn basic computer procedures and programming languages and create sets of tools and routines. For most historians, this latter option was extremely time-consuming, with most of the effort going into the software itself. Yet the fact that some historians did make the effort meant that there now exists a small group of highly proficient computing historians who have been able to develop, or encourage others to develop, a range of software tools specifically with the historian in mind. One of the most exciting of these is the Kleio software system developed by Manfred Thaller and his colleagues at Göttingen, which offers for the first time a package of well-documented and highly flexible source-oriented procedures which cover most of the material the historian wishes to use, from free text and statistical data to visual images. The ability to link and cross-reference a variety of different databases, moreover, which is an important feature of Kleio, offers the prospect for the real integration of machine-readable historical sources and thus the enhancement of the scholar's research horizons.

In the meantime, one consequence of using computers is that historians are forced to confront more directly such methodological issues as the structure of source material, the consistency of data and the relationship between parts of a source and the whole (Thaller, 1989a, 1989b). In the past, given that historians recognized the impossibility of exploring all the available source material, a form of paradigm analysis evolved by which historical explanation could be predicated on a judicious selection of examples. This is not to suggest that historians were in any way dishonest, but it was always very difficult to retrace all the steps taken from research to publication and this often forced historians into conducting debates through surrogate evidence: 'my example is more relevant than yours'. Computers, however, have changed the context in which research is conducted by providing transportable versions of source material. Not only can the archive come to the historian, but historians can confront each other's source material more fully than ever before. On the way, issues such as standardization and communication become central to the historiography. In the meantime, the work of creating the necessary databanks is moving ahead rapidly, although each step forward seems only to highlight the enormity of the task. At the same time one should not overstate the degree to which historians in the main have come to terms with these new opportunities.

There is another point. Even if historians find it difficult to organize and finance the conversion of their source material into machine-readable corpora, society itself has no such inhibitions. Our present is a computer-present and the history of our present will be dominated by the influence, as well as informed by the output, of computers. Ensuring the representative character of such material is a major concern for archivists as well as historians who have any sense of responsibility for future generations of their profession.

Technology itself is advancing in directions which offer exciting prospects for the humanities (Denley, 1990; Denley and Hopkin, 1990; Hopkin, 1991). The next generation of hypermedia, the relentless march of electronic communication, the increasing demand by historians for dedicated and appropriate source-oriented data processing software, and the development of image processing, offer invaluable additions to the already impressive range of technological tools. Historians are learning to make their own informed and confident demands on the technology instead of gathering the crumbs from the scientific or commercial table.

It is vital, however, to reassert the indivisibility of scholarship with teaching. The impact of computers on the teaching of history is not entirely clear. Much effort and money has been spent on the organizational infrastructure, and some important initiatives have been taken, notably in the United Kingdom, with the recent creation of a national centre for teaching computing in History at Glasgow and important local initiatives such as the HIDES project at Southampton (Morgan and Trainor, 1990). The problem is the degree to which an essentially mechanical instrument can be integrated with a traditionally eclectic and individuated pedagogy. Explorations of 'expert' systems in history understandably raise eyebrows among those who believe that historical expertise has little to do with epistemological certainty and may even be inversely related to it. Nevertheless, a profession which has consistently argued that its educational relevance is based on the skills it imparts as much as the knowledge it instills cannot run away from the technological imperatives of contemporary society. If the bureaucrats of the future are to be computer-literate, history students of the present must be taught computing.

There are signs, therefore, that the culture of the historian's work is being fundamentally altered. As individuals, historians are making ever greater use of computer technology for manuscript preparation and publication, thus expediting the processes of writing. An increasing number of historians have progressed to the next stage, using computers in a more substantial and far-reaching way, for database management, analysis and beyond. The discourse between technologically-minded historians and the rest is becoming easier as the common stock of terms and assumptions expands.

How great an impact has all this had on the general discipline of history and the perspectives of historians? The simplest answer is that which Chinese Premier Zhou En-lai gave to the question of what significance he attached to the French Revolution. His reported reply was 'It's too soon to tell'.

Structure

The inhibiting factor is the profession itself, not so much in its attitude as in its structure. In the British case, if this is the age of the greatest number of professional historians, it is also the age in which there are the fewest number of young historians, certainly in proportional terms. Much has been said about the impact on the structure of the historical profession of a decade of financial retrenchment. The serious part is not the retrenchment itself, but the way it has arbitrarily confined the profession to what might be called an interquartile range, deprived of the patriarchs and the apprentices, both of whom are probably as likely as not to be the most productive and fertile. We could go back and explore the reasons for this. We may even conclude that the expansion of higher education in the 1960s was damaging to the historical profession, in the UK certainly, because it was unsustainable. In the UK, for example, it consisted of an attempt to graft mass education onto the elitist structures of the past, but at an insensate speed and scale. One consequence was the clogging up of the historical profession so that over the last decade opportunities for young historians have been few and far between; there is now a lost generation of historians.

What it has meant, however, is an artificial restriction on the arrival of new ideas. So, for example, a society in which the main currency of politics is image creation has not yet got a body of historians either interested in or skilled in analyzing the processes of such image making. Our political history is still confined to the pre-media age of hustings, campaigning, even political issues. The advent of political agnosticism, if the opinion polls are anything to go by, has not yet got its historical equivalent.

Despite the frequent prophecies of gloom there are real glimmers of hope. Perhaps the real problem for historians arose with the advent of professionalism in the late nineteenth century and the imposition of a combination of stricter methodological rules and a greater reliance on remote archival resources which effectively prevented all but the best resourced scholars, in terms of time as well as finance, to undertake research and to publish their results. Computer-based resources, however, have the potential to break through the walls of institutions and through their associated constraints, such as access. The barriers between professional and amateur may yet begin to come down.

The other hope is for a rapid change in the balance within the profession. Sooner or later, there has to be an influx of new historians. It has been estimated that some 1,200 university historians will be needed by the year 2010 in Britain alone just to maintain the present reduced profession—that is approximately 50 new scholars each year on average, though in reality the distribution is much more uneven. It does not test the imagination too much to contemplate what will happen if there is no planned policy for postgraduate study which offers realistic opportunities for young historians within the profession. Nor should one forget those who have so far missed out, the lost generation of historians. The danger, of course, is that it will be a fearful scramble. If the work of the admirable History at the Universities Defence Group succeeds, however, the process may be moderated. In this case HUDG may come to be seen less as an academic equivalent of the World Wildlife Fund, in Cannadine's provocative phrase (1987ii), more the intellectual counterpart of the National Trust.

Conclusion

If concern for a state of a person's health is an indication of true charity, then history should be glad of the constant temperature-taking. But the wider role of history may well be in a state of improvement. Recent political events in Eastern Europe have underlined the need for a greater awareness of historical time and context. Isaac Deutscher's much vaunted Unfinished Revolution may, in retrospect, soon be seen never to have properly begun (Deutscher, 1967). Suddenly 1917 does not seem so far away, while the search for answers, in Lithuania as elsewhere, takes us well back through the nineteenth century and beyond. Even in Britain, there has been recognition that education is incomplete without history, even if there is some dispute over what that history should be or, indeed, who should control it.

For the historian, the arrival of technologies of bulk processing and rapid distribution, not to mention mass and selective communication, amount to a potential revolution for methodology and perception. Whether the historian, or scholars in any other discipline for that matter, can rise to the new challenges depends as much on education and training as on cross-fertilization with younger and different people.

In future there will be more of everything more readily and completely available than ever. The problem will be to avoid confusing *avoirdupois* with substance.

References

Bender, T. (1985) Making history whole again. **New York Times Book Reviews**, 6 October 1985.

Cannadine, D. (1987) British history: past, present—and future. **Past and Present**, 116, (i) p. 180; (ii) p. 181.

Clark, J.C.D. (1982) **The Dynamics of Change: The Crisis of the 1750s and the English Party System**. Cambridge: Cambridge University Press.

Computer applications in the historical sciences: selected contributions to the Cologne Computer Conference, (1988) **Historical Social Research**, 14:3 (1989); 14:4 (1989); 15:1 (1990).

Cooke, A.B. and Vincent, J. (1974) **The Governing Passion: Cabinet Government and Party Politics in Britain**, 1885-6. London: Harvester.

Cross, P.R., Lamont, W. and Evans, N. (1988) Debate: British history: past, present—and future? **Past and Present**, 119, 171-203.

Darnton, R. (1984) **The Great Cat Massacre**. London: Allen Lane.

Davies, R.R. (1987) **Conquest, Coexistence and Change. Wales, 1063-1415**, (i) p. 143. Oxford: Clarendon Press.

Denley, P. (1984) The use of computers in historical research. In **The Use of the Computer in the Study and Teaching of History**, edited by K. Randell, pp. 22-30. London: Historical Association.

Denley, P. and Hopkin, D. (1987) Editors. **History and Computing**. Manchester: Manchester University Press.

Denley, P., Harvey, C. and Fogelvik, S. (1989) Editors. **History and Computing II**. Manchester: Manchester University Press.

Denley, P. (1990) The computer revolution and 'redefining the humanities'. In **Humanities and the Computer. New Directions**, edited by D.S. Miall, pp. 13-25. Oxford: Oxford University Press.

Denley, P. and Hopkin, D. (1991, in press) Structures and strategies in historical computing. In **Arts Researchers on Computers**, edited by C.R.R. Turk. New York: Chapman and Hall.

Deutscher, I. (1967) **The Unfinished Revolution**. Oxford: Oxford University Press.

Elton, G.R. (1969) **The Practice of History**, (i) p. 20. London: Fontana.

Fieldhouse, D.K. (1983-84) Can Humpty Dumpty be put together again? Imperial History in the 1980s. **Journal of Imperial and Commonwealth Studies**, 12:2, 9-23.

Gardiner, J. (1988) Editor. **What is History Today?** London: Macmillan.

Gervers, M. (1987) The DEEDS project and a survey of the Essex textile industry in the twelfth and thirteenth centuries. In Denley and Hopkin (1987) 81-89.

Hopkin, D. (1990) Keeping up to date. **The Times Higher Education Supplement**, 15 June 1990.

International Review of Periodical Literature (1989).

Jarausch, K.H., Arminger, G. and Thaller, M. (1985) **Quantitative Methoden in der Geschichtwissenschaften.** Darmstadt: Wissenschaftliche Buchgesellschaft.

Le Roy Ladurie, E. (1981) **Carnival at Romans.** London: Penguin.

Lowenthal, D. (1985) **The Past is a Foreign Country,** (i) p. 411. Cambridge: Cambridge University Press.

Mawdsley, E., Morgan, N., Richmond,L. and Trainor, R. (1990) Editors. **History and Computing III.** Manchester: Manchester University Press.

Millet, H. (1985) Editor. **Informatique et prosopographie.** Paris: Editions du CNRS.

Morgan N.J. and Trainor, R.H. (1990) Liberator or libertine? The computer in the history classroom. In **Humanities and the Computer. New Directions,** edited by D.S. Miall, pp. 61-70. Oxford: Oxford University Press.

Pouyez, C. et al. (1983) **Les Saguenayens. Introduction à l'histoire de la population du Saguenay, XVe-XXe siécles.** Québec: Presses de l'Université.

Rabb, T.K. and Rotberg, R.I. (1982) Editors. **The New History: The 1980s and Beyond.** Princeton, NJ: Princeton University Press.

Reconstitution automatique des familles. Le systéme de SOREP (1988). 2 vols. Québec: Presses de l'Université.

Schama, S. (1977) **Patriots and Liberators: Revolution in the Netherlands,** 1780-1813. London: Collins.

Schama, S. (1988) **The Embarrassment of Riches: An Interpretation of Dutch Culture in the Golden Age.** London: Collins.

Schama, S. (1989) **Citizens. A Chronicle of the French Revolution.** London: Viking.

Scribner, R.W. (1987) **Popular Culture and Popular Movements in Reformation Germany.** London: Hambledon.

Speck, W.A. and Gray, W.A. (1970) Computer analysis of poll books: an initial report. **Bulletin of the Institute of Historical Research**, 43, 105-12.

Speck, W.A., Gray, W.A. and Hopkinson, R. (1975) Computer analysis of poll books: a further report. **Bulletin of the Institute of Historical Research**, 48, 64-90

Stern, F. (1956) Editor. **The Varieties of History. From Voltaire to the Present**. London: Macmillan.

Stone, L. (1987) **The Past and the Present Revisited**, (i) p. xi; (ii) p. 74. London: Routledge.

Thaller, M. (1989a) The need for a theory of historical computing. In Denley, Harvey and Fogelvik (1989), 2-11.

Thaller, M. (1989b) Warum brauchen die Geschichtswissenschaften fachspezifische datentechnische Lösungen? Das Beispiel kontextsensitiver Datenbanken. In **Computer in den Geisteswissenschaften. Konzepte und Berichte**, edited by M. Thaller and A. Müller, pp. 237-64. Ludwig-Boltzmann-Institut für Historische Sozialwissenschaft: Studien zur Historischen Sozialwissenschaft: Frankfurt/New York, Campus Verlag.

Thernstrom, S. (1973) **The Other Bostonians**, (i) p. 268. Cambridge, Mass.: Harvard University Press.

Thomas, K.V. (1971) **Religion and the Decline of Magic**. London: Weidenfeld.

Thomas, K.V. (1983) **Man and his Natural World. Changing Attitudes in England 1500-1800**. London: Allen Lane.

Tosh, J. (1984) **The Pursuit of History**, (i) p. 192. London: Longman.

Wakelin, P. (1987) Comprehensive computerisation of a very large documentary source: the Portbooks Project at Wolverhampton Polytechnic. In Denley and Hopkin (1987) 109-115.

Wrigley, E.A. and Schofield, R.S. (1981) **The Population History of England**, 1541-1831. London: Arnold.

Connected Images: Hypermedia and the Future of Art Historical Studies

George P. Landow
Brown University

Modern art history requires photography, to be sure, but print, the dominant information technology of the past four centuries, has produced art historical and other humanistic scholarship as we know it. We may expect that new information technologies that have the fundamental impact of print will in turn change the conception and practice of the art historian's enterprise. Computer hypermedia, which produces texts in ways that differ fundamentally from those created by printing, therefore offers the promise or threat of thus changing the conception and practice of art history. All the effects of computing derive from its fundamental shift in the way we record, store, and manipulate information—from, in other words, the electronic medium's replacement of fixed physical records composed of pigment on paper, film, or some other surface by electronic records in digitally encoded form. Where information is concerned, availability is not equivalent to accessibility, and digital technology makes visual, verbal, and other forms of information both far more accessible and far easier to manipulate.

After examining some of the implications of digitizing information for art historians and other scholars, I shall look at the natural extension of such information technology into electronic hypertext and hypermedia, whose defining attributes lie in their linking together of data.

Because videodisc technology exemplifies the ways digitized information increases the scholar's ability to access information quickly, it provides a convenient entrance to our subject. Using a videodisc on which colour images have been stored in the form of digital coding (or digitized), an art historian can use information in ways impossible either with print technology or videotape. These new possibilities arise because digitized technology permits virtually instant retrieval of images or other data anywhere on a disc since a search brings one directly to the location (the address) of an image rather than requiring a sequential scan through hundreds or even thousands of them. Videodiscs already exist for entire museum collections, and one readily envisages placing entire oeuvres of single artists or of entire schools on them. When combined with computer technology, such videodiscs permit the art historian to work with images much as classicists now work with texts. Putting on a single compact disc the entire *Thesaurus Linguae Graecae*, which contains more than 95 per cent of all archaic and classical Greek texts, has permitted classicists to relate any particular word or phrase to its every occurrence in ancient Greek (Kahn, 1986). This capacity to create customized word lists has enabled scholars to investigate particularly thorny problems in dating, attribution, stylistic development, and translation. Electronic computing has dramatically amplified the range of problems scientists can tackle, and it has already begun to have the same effect on the humanistic disciplines.

Videodisc technology, which tantalizes the art historian by its promise of near-instant access to visual information, nonetheless represents only a crude and costly hint of things to come because it retains some of the basic limitations of book technology. In particular, present videodiscs require a separate player for each user, and they also require frequent physical changing of them since any individual disc, particularly those produced as catalogues by individual institutions, contains a necessarily limited amount of information. For example, even if there existed videodisc records of the Tate Gallery and the Manchester City Art Gallery collections, anyone working with, say, the relationship of Early Netherlandish painting and nineteenth-century Pre-Raphaelitism would either have to change videodiscs frequently—or have access to a system with several videodisc players working in tandem. Furthermore, the information on these discs provides only a resource for scholarly reference, not one for writing or for publication, since present videodisc technology does not permit the art historian to incorporate materials from a videodisc into his own finished publication.

The solution to many of these problems involves creating more efficient means of storing and retrieving digitized information of the kind already contained on videodiscs. Essentially, one must do for visual information what one already does for verbal information—store it in a central repository (database) that can then share it among many readers by means of a network that joins this database and the devices (terminals) on which readers examine verbal and graphic information. The great, defining power of digital technology lies in its capacity to store information and provide countless virtual versions of it to readers, who then can manipulate, copy, and comment upon it without changing the material seen by others. When combined with electronic networks, digitized information technology produces a new kind of information medium in which reading, writing, and publication take on new characteristics (Bolter, 1989, 1990; Heim, 1987).

Networks capable of limited versions of such information exchange already exist within individual laboratories, classrooms, and libraries and throughout entire universities. As the technology improves, one can expect that such networks capable of interactive computing (as opposed to batch processing) will stretch across oceans and continents to join universities, museums, libraries, and other institutions around the world—as BITNET already does for purposes of electronic mail and data transfer. Such networks will permit the relatively efficient sharing of information and the creation of a new kind of scholarship.

Hypertext and hypermedia are the natural extensions of digitizing information. Theodor H. Nelson coined the term *hypertext* in the 1960s to refer to text in an electronic medium designed to be read nonsequentially or in a nonlinear manner (Nelson, 1981; Conklin, 1987); *hypermedia* simply extends the concept to include visual and other forms of information, such as sound and motion. One can easily comprehend what is meant by nonlinear (or multilinear) reading if one recalls how an art historian proceeds through a scholarly article in his or her field. In reading an article on, say, William Holman Hunt's *Shadow of Death*, one reads through the main text, encounters a symbol that indicates the presence of a footnote, and leaves the main text to read that note, which can contain a citation of passages in the artist's own exhibition pamphlet that supposedly support the argument in question as well as information about sources, influences, historical background, or related articles. In each case, the reader can follow the link to another text and thus move entirely outside the scholarly article itself. Having completed reading the note—and perhaps leaving the article entirely to consult some of the texts or images to which it refers—one returns to the main text and continues reading until one encounters another note and again leaves the main text.

This kind of reading constitutes the model for hypertext. Suppose now that one could simply touch the page at the point where the symbol of a note, reference, or annotation appeared, and that act instantly brought into view the material contained in a note or even the entire text to which it refers, say, exhibition catalogues, contemporary reviews, or modern scholarly articles and books. Scholarly articles situate themselves by means of notes within a field of relations, most of which the print medium keeps out of sight and relatively difficult to follow because the referenced (or linked) materials lie spatially distant from the reference mark. Electronic hypertext, in contrast, makes individual references easy to follow and the entire field of interconnections obvious and easy to navigate.

Hypertext, the next stage of digitized information, is at one and the same time a form of electronic text, an instantiation of many ideas of Roland Barthes (Barthes, 1974), a radically new information technology, a mode of publication, and a resource for collaborative work. 'Both an author's tool and a reader's medium, a hypertext document system allows authors or groups of authors to link information together, create paths through a corpus of related material, annotate existing texts, and create notes that point readers to either bibliographic data or the body of the referenced text... Readers can browse through linked, cross-referenced, annotated texts in an orderly but nonsequential manner' (Yankelovich, Meyrowitz and van Dam, 1985). Such electronic linking shifts the boundaries between individual works as well as those between author and reader and between teacher and student. Demanding new forms of rhetoric (Landow, 1989c) and new educational applications (Landow, 1989b), it also has radical effects upon our experience of author, text, and work, revealing that many of our most cherished, most commonplace ideas and attitudes of literary production are the result of the particular technology of information that has provided the setting for them (Landow, 1989a).

Changing the ease with which one can orient oneself within such a context in order to pursue individual references radically changes both the experience of reading and ultimately the nature of that which is read. For example, if one possessed a hypertext system in which our putative article existed linked to all the other materials it cited, it would exist as part of a much larger system in which the totality might count more than the individual document; the article would now appear woven more tightly into its context than would a print-technology counterpart. As one might expect, the fact that one writes in the presence of earlier authors on one's subject transforms one's work into a kind of electronic collaboration (Landow, 1990a).

Hypertext adds to book technology a new flexibility and accessibility and thereby promises to change the scholarly process. As Ivins (1953) and Eisenstein (1979) have pointed out, the fixed texts and images that print technology generated have produced much of what we understand by scholarship. In the first place, print, by reproducing a fixed text in multiple copies, permits readers widely separated spatially and temporally to locate precisely the same passage, image, or other data. On the one hand, printed reproductions provide a fixed text in multiple copies that scholars in different times and places can cite efficiently. On the other hand, the very strengths create certain problems. In particular, book technology creates a form of recording and storing images that makes them difficult to locate and difficult to relate to texts and other visual information.

In addition to the obvious expense of obtaining and maintaining reproduced images of individual works of art both in preliminary research and in eventual publication, such reproductions present the researcher with other problems related to book technology. Even if including all possible relevant images needed for a particular subject proved economically feasible, the user of that book still faces two fundamental problems: first, the resultant volume would be too large, too heavy for convenient use and storage; second, the resulting volume, no matter how lavishly illustrated, still permits the reader to consult reproductions appearing on only one set of pages at a time. Anyone who has worked with visual information will remember how one inserts one's fingers, bookmarks, and anything else at hand to mark one's place. At times one resorts to several volumes with illustrations of the same work so that one will not have to close one book and lose sight of a particular image. Such experiences convince one that the art historian needs a means of working with images—visual data—that make their locations both more readily accessible and more adaptable for use in multiple contexts. As we shall see, hypertext, which permits multiple connections and multiple rapid retrieval of images, answers this need.

Another related limitation of present technologies of image reproduction similarly involves their fixity, and again digitizing information offers a better solution. No matter how accurate the information colour transparencies and black and white reproductions provide, they provide that information only from a single, fixed vantage point and only in a single, fixed scale. In contrast, digital technology permits one to record multiple images of three-dimensional work so that the reader, who can now interact with his text, obtains dynamic, multiple views such as the Harvard University Project Perseus has created for Classical Greek art. No longer confined to one spatial point of view or to a single scale, the art historian can make a bronze or a piece of pottery revolve or present detailed views of particular parts.

Present technology requires video display terminals linked to computers, but in the future one expects that such reproduction will not find itself limited to screens. In fact, one easily envisages holographic, variable size images that would permit the art historian to place an object within a variety of settings. One could, for example, examine objects full-size and within their actual conditions at various times in their history. Furthermore, one could examine individual works with varying lighting, contrast, and vantage points so that one could study, say, Michelangelo's Sistine Chapel from the spatial position of several viewers as well as from one closer to the object. With such technology, which would also permit the art historian to experience objects as they appear at different historical moments, one could examine works within varying contexts provided by changing settings, conditions of the object, and so on. I must emphasize that although such a scenario might seem little more than science-fiction speculation, in fact much of the necessary technology already exists for military and related applications, such as training commercial pilots, and workers in the field have already carried out rudimentary applications for art education and entertainment (Zachary, 1990).

A third major limitation of book technology involves the limited connectivity of books. For all their advantages, books have two problems intimately related directly to their strengths, strengths that derive from a fixed, physically isolated text. First, ordering information in an essentially linear stream of language makes finding any particular bit of that information difficult unless one reads through the entire text or major section of it. In the early Middle Ages, scribes began to place symbols in the margins of manuscripts to indicate chapter divisions, but hundreds of years passed before they used interword spacing. Since the invention of printing, publishers, book designers, and authors have developed far more elaborate systems for retrieving information, including tables of contents, indices, pagination, footnotes, publication data, and bibliographies. Nonetheless, although the printed book represents an enormous improvement on the manuscript scroll or codex, it, like the codex, still is ill-suited to retrieving or locating specific bits of information from the text stream (Bolter, 1990).

Equally important, the physically separate text similarly hinders our perceiving connections—connections between texts and other texts, between texts and images, and between images and other images. Over the centuries authors have therefore developed devices of intertextual and intratextual reference. In addition, scholarly devices, such as footnotes and bibliographical references, have also developed to provide means of referring to materials found outside the main text. All such devices situate the individual text within a network of relations. Notes thus serve as stage directions, instructions about performance, for when encountering these behavioural cues, we receive instructions to leave the text we are currently reading and consult another one. The electronic linking that defines hypertext (or hypermedia) reifies such indicated relations and in effect draws the texts closer together. In addition, both because electronic hypertext linking does not have to be as obtrusive as footnotes or endnotes and because it works vastly more quickly, it permits far more annotation.

Having discussed hypertext only in general terms, I propose now to describe how an art historian would use Intermedia, perhaps the most advanced current hypertext system. Intermedia, which Brown University's Institute for Research in Information and Scholarship (IRIS) developed with assistance from IBM, Apple Computer, and the Annenberg/CPB Project, has been extensively described elsewhere in technical detail and with copious illustration (Yankelovich *et al.*, 1988; Landow, 1989a; Utting and Yankelovich, 1989). I shall therefore confine myself to narrating a brief scenario that shows how an art historian specializing in nineteenth-century Britain works with the system currently in use at Brown University's IRIS and in a classroom at the university's computer centre.

After logging onto one of twenty-four Apple Macintosh II computers that run A/UX, Apple's version of the UNIX operating system, one types the command 'Intermedia'. After a minute or so a dozen icons in the shape of file folders appear. At this point one uses a mouse to activate and then open the folder labelled 'Visual Arts'. (If, on the other hand, one wished to begin by investigating some aspect of Victorian social history or literature, one could begin by opening folders labelled 'History' or 'English'). One next decides which set of links to activate. Choosing '*Context32*', our art historian double-clicks upon it and then waits a minute or two for that action to generate the 2,500 electronic links that bind together the more than 1,000 documents. When this set of links, or web, becomes active, a window entitled 'Context32: Web View' appears at the right side of the monitor's screen (Figure 1), providing a

Figure 1: *(left side of screen)*

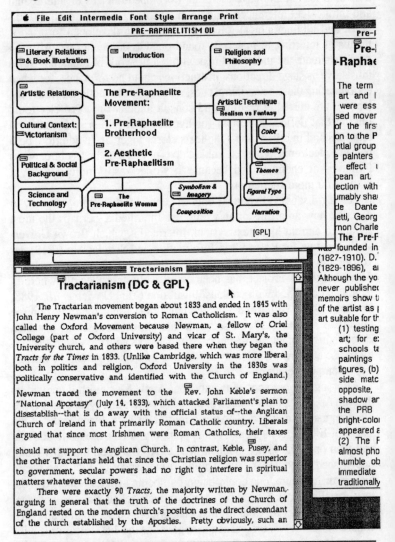

sequence of icons representing the documents examined during our scholar's last session. (One effect of logging on—or entering—Intermedia as an individual with one's own password is that such a manner of

Figure 1 continued: (right side of screen)

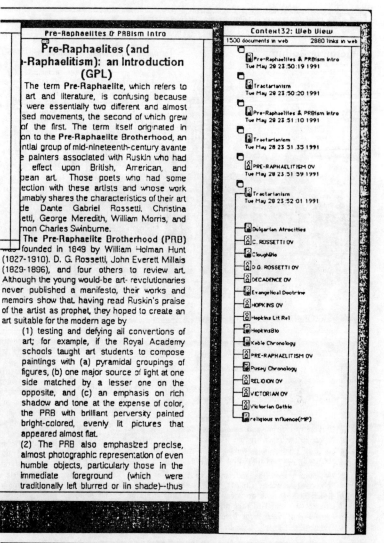

proceeding not only allows privacy and protects one's documents but also permits the system to provide one with a history of one's recent work.) If one wishes, one can return to any of these documents by

Figure 2: (left side of screen)

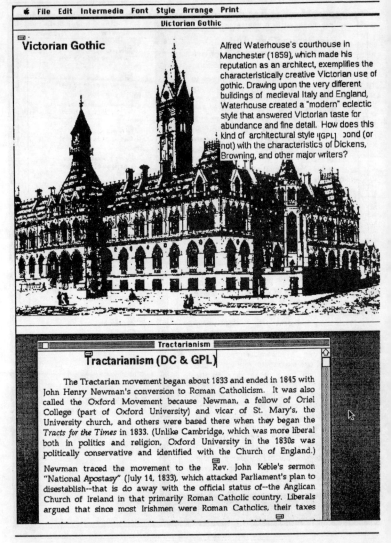

clicking twice upon the icon that represents it. Since our scholar wishes to work with the English Pre-Raphaelites, but she had last been reading documents about Alfred Waterhouse's Manchester law courts, she does

***Figure 2 continued:** (right side of screen)*

not employ the web view at this point but instead opens a folder for
nineteenth-century British painting and then one inside that labelled
'Pre-Raphaelites'.

Inside this folder she finds several dozen labelled icons representing graphic and textual documents. Since she wishes first to review some of the documents she and other scholars have placed in this folder, she follows the usual procedure and opens one of several overview files. Choosing that entitled 'PRE-RAPHAELITISM OV'—overview or directory files appear in full caps to make them easier to find—she comes upon a diagram that indicates the kinds of information immediately available about a particular artist, subject, or movement. Following a standard paradigm, the overview for Pre-Raphaelitism surrounds a centre labelled 'The Pre-Raphaelite Movement' with boxes indicating the presence of information on political and social background, religion and philosophy, science and technology, cultural context (Victorianism), literary relations, artistic relations, and so forth. Looking now at the web view that appears on the right side of the screen, one discovers that it has transformed itself into a row of icons indicating the several dozen documents directly linked to the overview. One can open these documents either by clicking on the label in the overview, each of which can lead to as many as 100 documents and images, or by choosing one in the web view on the right. These documents take the form of primary and secondary sources, digitized images (Figure 2), timelines, bibliographies, and so on, most of which were developed for use in a range of undergraduate and graduate courses at Brown University (Landow, 1989a).

The flexibility of the system, however, has proved to narrow the separation between research and class preparation rather dramatically since faculty members can easily draw upon materials of current projects for their teaching—a process made convenient by the ability of Intermedia to accept materials written in several common wordprocessing languages. Our art historian wishes to work on a planned article and not on course materials, and so using the features already described, she calls up various Pre-Raphaelite paintings and woodcuts illustrating Tennyson's 'Lady of Shalott'; because Intermedia permits one to open an indefinite number of documents at the same time, she can juxtapose these versions, duplicate any one of them and mark them with her own compositional and iconographical analyses, and finally link them to any of her own or other author's documents. She can also copy passages from secondary materials on the system or annotate them for her own purposes.

Looking at William Holman Hunt's large version of the subject, which is now in Hartford, Connecticut, our art historian wishes to determine how closely the lady's discarded clogs resemble those in paintings by van Eyck and Memling, so she searches through folders until she finds reproductions of the relevant works. Then, using Intermedia's recently developed capacity to permit full-text searches, she uses the computer mouse to begin one (Coombs, 1990). When a dialogue box appears, she types 'Hunt Van Eyck Memling composition' and after waiting twenty to thirty seconds, she receives a hierarchically arranged list of all documents on Intermedia (whether or not they appear in the *Context32* web) in which these terms appear; those documents discussing composition in all three artists receive highest weighting, those discussing three of the four terms appear next, and so on. Opening several of the most promising documents, which turn out to be passages from recent books and essays, she decides to link them to her own notes. One creates a link by highlighting a passage or image by holding down the mouse button and then using it to move the cursor across the desired passages. Once they have become highlighted, one requests 'start link' from the Intermedia menu at the top of the screen, moves to the other end of the desired link, and repeats this action. Upon requesting 'complete link' from the Intermedia menu, a marker indicating the new link appears at the beginning of each linked passage of text and icons for the link and newly linked document appear in the web view.

Clearly, working in a hypertext environment permits the scholar to obtain information far more rapidly than has been otherwise possible (assuming, of course, that the textual or visual information appears on the system), and it also permits the scholar to make annotations, comments, and working notes. Most important, a hypermedia environment allows art historians far more easily to do what a recent study suggests is their primary scholarly act—perceiving, recording, and analyzing relations among large amounts of data (Bakewell *et al.*, 1988).

Intermedia already provides full-text searching of documents. A future system truly adapted to the needs of art historians would solve the far more difficult problem of extending to visual information this search capacity. Of course, if one appends verbal tags to images either in the form of titles, captions, and appended commentary or in the form of keywords, one can employ Intermedia-style full-text searches to produce lists of relevant images. Such a procedure, however, represents merely a crude, if extremely helpful, stopgap since it requires preliminary tagging of a corpus of images, analogous to that for each image in the *Princeton*

Index of Christian Art. True full-image searches, in contrast, do not require an initial—and hence confining—categorization that may later prove inadequate to the needs of later researchers.

Such image searches for purposes of compositional, iconographical, and iconological analyses require pattern recognition, a capacity also crucial to robotics, machine translation, and various scientific applications, such as the automatic counting and classification of micro-organisms. Computer pattern recognition, which remains at a rudimentary stage, in turn demands—or seems to demand—some form of artificial intelligence (McCorduck, 1979). When computer scientists manage to achieve reliable automatic matching of shape, tonality, colour, and texture, art historians will be able to take advantage of such a capacity to screen enormous numbers of images and objects. An art historian interested in nineteenth-century adaptations of the annunciation theme could choose a sample work, say, Burne-Jones's version of the subject, and then have the computer search for similar disposition of figures in other works by the painter as well as those by other artists. Such a search, which would provide examples of the artist's characteristic use of a narrow vertical canvas in nonreligious subjects, could combine with various parameters to suggest developments in the painter's style and themes. Like a colour slide, xerographic reproduction, or pad and pencil, the computer allows the scholar to process data more quickly and to record her conclusions. However much this machine becomes an intellectual prosthesis, it still requires a human mind to direct it and to take advantage of its assistance.

In conclusion, then, we may ask ourselves how hypertext will change art history and other scholarship, and we can answer that any information technology that has the potential to permit the scholar to obtain large amounts of relevant information quickly and easily will change the nature of scholarly work. Eisenstein (1979) points out that by combining reproducibility (or the fact of multiple copies) with a fixed text, printing created an entirely new means of preserving text, image, and information that changed the scholar's role. This change in ideas about how to preserve knowledge directly affected how scholars conceived of their enterprise: Scholars in a manuscript culture protected their information by squirrelling it away and restricting access (since each use of a manuscript shortens its life and necessitates recopying it with inevitable attendant scribal error). In contrast, the technology of print created the idea that one preserves information by disseminating it.

Print technology's mode of preserving and disseminating information led to radical changes in the scholar's enterprise. Whereas scholars in a manuscript culture conceived it as their main task to involve the preservation of fragile texts, those working in print culture expend far more time on the criticism and connection of these texts. One can predict that hypertext has the potential to create equally significant changes in scholarship. In particular, an information technology that thus stresses connectivity promises to privilege those scholarly and critical tasks in which establishing or perceiving relationships plays a central role. Furthermore, since hypermedia allows linking of entire primary and secondary works, conventions about reference, quotation, and citation will change, and this same electronic intertextuality, which immediately blurs the boundary of individual texts, alters basic notions of supposedly independent, self-sufficient works just as it alters—in fact erodes—conceptions of authorial property, originality, and creativity. In scholarly terms, these changes imply a greater recognition of the collaborative nature of research and scholarly contribution, and they may also therefore lead to new emphasis on group or collaborative production of texts. Finally, since publication will come to mean gaining access to a particular electronic network or networks, the conception of publication as act and legal entity will also change.

Because hypertext adds the link, a new component, to text, it can change the very conception of writing and composition (Yankelovich, Meyrowitz and van Dam, 1985). Within such a new form of writing (and publication) creating a link appears just as much an act of composition or of writing as does creating sentences and paragraphs. Work with existing hypermedia systems demonstrates that from a common set of texts (or metatext) different authors create different documents or document sets by linking differently (Landow, 1990b). Thus, at Brown University, texts created to provide information for advanced students of cell biology, international affairs, and the history of public health have been linked by later authors to materials for students of nineteenth- and twentieth-century fiction. Drawing upon this experience, we can expect that basic scholarship, like the preparation of teaching materials, will take the form of producing sets of links that radically reinterpret previously available information.

Many of the effects of hypermedia derive from its creating what we may term the *virtual presence* of all the authors who contribute to its materials. Using an analogy to optics, computer scientists speak of 'virtual machines' created by an operating system that provides individual users with the experience of working on their own individual machines when they in fact share a system with as many as several hundred others. Computing makes great use of this kind of virtuality: since text processing is a matter of manipulating computer-manipulated codes, all texts that the writer encounters on the screen are virtual, rather than real, texts in two senses. First, according to conventional usage, they only become texts when printed on paper in so-called hard copy; second, once a writer places some portion of that text in the computer's memory, any work upon that text encounters a virtual text in another sense—the original resides in memory and one works on an electronic copy until such time as the two converge when the text is 'saved' by placing the changes in memory. At this point, text in the reader and in memory coincide. In a similar manner, the reader experiences the virtual presence of other contributors.

Such virtual presence is, of course, a characteristic of all technology of cultural memory based on writing and symbol systems. Since we all manipulate cultural codes, particularly language but also mathematics and other symbols, in slightly different ways, each record of an utterance conveys a sense of the one who makes that utterance. Hypermedia differs from print technology, however, in several crucial ways that amplify this notion of virtual presence. Because the essential connectivity of hypermedia removes the physical isolation of individual texts in print technology, the presence of individual authors becomes both more available and more important.

References

Bakewell, E., Beeman, W.O., Reese, C.M. and Schmidt, M. (1988) **Object Image Inquiry: The Art Historian at Work.** Report on a Collaborative Study by the Getty Art History Information Program (AHIP) and the Institute for Research in Information and Scholarship (IRIS), Brown University. Santa Monica, California: Getty Art History Information Program.

Barthes, R. (1974) **S/Z**, translated by R. Miller. New York: Hill and Wang.

Bolter, J.D. (1989) Beyond wordprocessing: the computer as a new writing space. **Language and Communication**, 9, 129-142.

Bolter, J.D. (1990) **Writing Space: The Computer in the History of Literacy.** Hillsdale, NJ: Lawrence Erlbaum.

Conklin, J. (1987) Hypertext: an introduction and survey. **IEEE Computer,** 19, 17-41.

Coombs, J.H. (1990) **Hypertext, Full Text, and Automatic Linking.** Technical Report. Providence, Rhode Island: Brown University, Institute for Research in Information and Scholarship.

Eisenstein, E.L. (1979) **The Printing Press as an Agent of Change: Communications and Cultural Transformations in Early Modern Europe,** 2 vols. Cambridge: Cambridge University Press.

Heim, M. (1987) **Electric Language: A Philosophical Study of Word Processing.** New Haven and London: Yale University Press.

Ivins, W. (1953) **Prints and Visual Communication.** London: Routledge & Kegan Paul; reprint New York: DaCapo, 1969.

Kahn, P.D. (1986) Isocrates: Greek literature on CD Rom. In **CD ROM: The New Papyrus: The Current and Future State of the Art,** edited by S. Lambert and S. Ropiequet. Redmond, Washington: Microsoft Press.

Landow, G.P. (1989a) Hypertext in literary education, criticism and scholarship. **Computers and the Humanities,** 23, 173-98.

Landow, G.P. (1989b) Course assignments using hypertext: the example of Intermedia. **Journal of Research in Computing in Education,** 21, 349-65.

Landow, G.P. (1989c) The rhetoric of hypermedia: some rules for authors. **Journal of Computing in Higher Education,** 1, 39-64.

Landow, G.P. (1990a) Hypertext and collaborative work: the example of Intermedia. In **Intellectual Teamwork,** edited by R. Kraut and J. Galegher. Hillsdale, NJ: Lawrence Erlbaum.

Landow, G.P. (1990b) Popular fallacies about hypertext. In **Designing Hypertext/Hypermedia for Learning,** edited by D.H. Jonassen and H. Mandl. Heidelberg: Springer-Verlag.

Landow, G.P. (1991) **Hypertext: the convergence of contemporary critical theory and technology.** Baltimore, Maryland: Johns Hopkins University Press.

McCorduck, P. (1979) **Machines Who Think: A Personal Inquiry into** the History and Prospects of Artificial Intelligence. New York: W.H. Freeman.

McLuhan, M. (1962) The Gutenberg Galaxy: The Making of Typographic Man. Toronto: University of Toronto Press.

Nelson, T.H. (1981) Literary Machines. Self-published: P.O. Box 128, Swarthmore, PA 19091.

Nelson, T.H. (1987) Computer Lib/Dream Machines. Seattle: Microsoft Press.

Utting, K. and Yankelovich, N. (1989) Context and orientation in hypermedia networks. ACM Transactions on Information Systems, 7, 58-84.

Yankelovich, N., Meyrowitz, N. and van Dam, A. (1985) Reading and writing the electronic book. IEEE Computer, 18, 15-30.

Yankelovich, N., Landow, G.P. and Cody, D. (1987) Creating hypermedia materials for English literature students. SIGCUE Outlook, 19, 12-25.

Yankelovich, N., Haan, B., Meyrowitz, N. and Drucker, S. (1988) Intermedia: the concept and the construction of a seamless information environment. IEEE Computer, 23, 81-96.

Zachary, G.P. (1990) Artificial reality: computer simulations one day may provide surreal experiences. Wall Street Journal, 23 January 1990, A1, A9.

The Impact of Computer-based Techniques on Research in Archaeology

J-C. Gardin

Centre National de la Recherche Scientifique

The subject of this paper can be approached in two ways according to which of its two facets is taken as a starting point. One may begin with an 'overview of the most important trends in research' in the discipline under study (quoted from one of the calls for contributions to this conference) and then examine the part played by technology in this evolution. Or we may consider first the applications of technology and then try to assess their effect on 'the content, methodology and style of research' in that discipline (*ibid.*). The former course seemed to me somewhat frightening: I felt unable to draw a fair picture of the new orientations of archaeological research in the last ten or fifteen years within the limits of time and space wisely imposed upon us. I have therefore chosen the second, undoubtedly easier course—easier for the simple reason that we need only consider then the subset of archaeological research that calls on technology.

Yet, a difficulty immediately arises: what do we mean by technology? Do we have in mind exclusively the so-called information technology (IT), as some of the announcements of this conference seemed to imply through their emphasis on 'computer-based methods'? Or should we take a broader view, and consider the wide range of techniques encompassed under the name of archaeometry as relevant to our purpose? I shall again choose the easier course, namely the former, but with some reservations: archaeology today is totally dependent upon a large variety of increasingly sophisticated techniques originating in the material or natural sciences—physics, chemistry, biology, etc. Indeed, research programmes that do *not* call upon such techniques, for some purpose or other (dating, provenance, identification of constituents or species, etc.), are now the exception. If technology were to be understood as referring indiscriminately to all kinds of laboratory tools in that broad sense, including both methods and equipment, the present paper would have to take the form of a survey of archaeometrical applications and their contributions to our knowledge of the past—which is not, I believe, in the spirit of this conference. However, computer-based methods are often associated with the analytical techniques developed under that name; also, some of the basic issues raised apropos of the proper use of computers or computing in the humanities apply to archaeometric studies as much as to any other, as we shall observe further on.

After having restricted our domain of exploration to IT, we are still left with an impressive variety of computer uses in archaeology, at different stages of the research process; handling large sets of data collected through modern survey techniques (geophysics, teledetection); holding excavation records; organizing material finds into meaningful orders; giving access to vast stores of information scattered in publications or collections from all over the world; cumulating the knowledge of experts in specific fields of research as an aid to interpretation; communicating selected pieces of information and knowledge to different categories of users, through computer-assisted educational programmes, etc.

The principles upon which such applications of computers are based are not specifically related to archaeology; parallels exist for each one of them in other disciplines—history, philosophy, literary and art studies—so that I need not dwell upon them in my particular context. The interesting question is whether we are in a position to evaluate their impact upon the processes or products of research in archaeology over the past ten or fifteen years.

I would not be bold enough to risk a global answer for archaeology as a whole. The use of IT is not evenly distributed throughout the world, nor among the various branches of archaeology (e.g. Classical, Amerindian, Medieval, etc.) in the more computer-oriented nations. Further, my coverage of the subject is also uneven, to say the least; I feel on firmer ground when discussing specific classes of computer applications with which I am more familiar than others, and for which I believe—rightly or wrongly—that the number of examples known to me is large enough to authorize some generalizations.

What do I mean by a specific class of computer applications? Essentially, a set of formal procedures intended to fulfil a unique function, however broadly defined, at any stage of the research process (the word 'formal' being here loosely understood as 'computable' without necessarily implying reference to mathematics or logic). The more ancient classes of computer application in that sense have to do with two well-established functions: information storage and retrieval, in any of its forms (bibliographic systems, archaeological databanks, excavation archives, museum catalogues, national or regional inventories, etc.), and ordering or classification, again in the broadest sense (typology, seriation, mathematical, networking, etc.). Let us examine the recent progress of computer technology in each case and its effect on archaeological research.

Information storage and retrieval (ISR)

The history of ISR applications in archaeology is long enough (over 30 years) to reveal interesting trends, which I would summarize as follows: In the late '50s and in the '60s, it was generally accepted that the major problem in the formalization of information or document searches lay in a proper control of the language in which the two sets of expressions involved ('data' and 'queries') were to be formulated, so as to maximize the efficiency of the matching process. References were then made to the need for artificial systems of description, more or less divorced from natural language, under a variety of names—standard lists of attributes or descriptors, information or documentary languages, semiological systems, codes, etc. Some of the promoters of such tools—including the present author—seemed to take for granted the feasibility of universal systems based on an Ars Combinatoria in the Leibnitzian sense. Experience soon brought home the inefficiency of that strategy as a practical proposition. Alternative paths were then envisaged, which are worth recalling, since they are still with us today, despite a number of reasons for regarding one or two of them with some suspicion.

The first one, in chronological order, was the strategy of 'searching in natural language' (NL), based on the idea that the growing power of computers made it unnecessary to go through the complicated and questionable process of representation in artificial information languages. As the fallacy of the argument emerged, it was reformulated more properly as a plea for the transformation of NL queries into various paraphrases or translations, under the control of the computer, so as to broaden the potential range of relevant answers. NL parsers and semantic tables of sorts are one way to achieve this goal; another way consists in adding a conversational component into the picture, thus leaving some of the linguistic decisions to the user. A number of information experts still seem to believe that modern strategies of that sort demonstrate that no representation systems or metalanguages are needed in the ISR process, contrary to the position taken thirty years ago. One would hope that scholars with a minimal of training in semantics would not fall into that trap.

The same misconception has, however, been recently revived by a superb technological innovation, namely compact memories (videodiscs, CD-ROMs, etc.). The potential of this tool is enormous in archaeology, as in most of the other humanistic disciplines, where 'facts', 'documents' or 'data' are scattered in thousands of libraries, museums and other warehouses of a less dignified sort. Being able to have at our fingertips all the texts inherited from ancient Greece, for instance—inscriptions, literary works or others—is undoubtedly a major contribution of IT to classical studies. Having access to all the known mosaics from Roman times on a single disc is no less an achievement. Only, we should again resist the claim sometimes made that such innovations mean the end of our concern for ISR issues: storage is one thing, for which compact memories are indeed revolutionary; retrieval is another, which these tools leave untouched. It is true that combinations of browsing and shallow indexing are sometimes regarded as sufficient; true also, strategies of that sort are generally presented as provisional, until more sophisticated tools are available for 'deep' retrieval. This, however, is but a tacit acknowledgement of the fact that representation issues are still with us today, unaltered, despite the remarkable progress of IT in the last decade.

'Unaltered'? Well, not necessarily. There now exists, largely as a consequence of the progress of information techniques, a sizeable body of experience and thought on matters of representation in scientific disciplines—archaeology among them. My contention is that it will become increasingly difficult to leave such matters out of our consideration when conducting scholarly work of any sort. A strong substantiation of that claim will be presented below, in relation to the progress of artificial intelligence (AI) techniques in archaeology (see '*Interpretations*' below).

Before we reach that point, let us consider the second class of computer applications mentioned above, under the broad title of ordering or classification.

Ordering

The use of computers to implement formal methods of ordering archaeological data also goes back to the late '50s. Applications of that sort have since multiplied to the point where they now form a distinct branch of archaeological research, with its own experts and literature. The formal methods in question were developed mostly prior to or independently of the computer; yet it is true that their application to relatively large bodies of data was especially due to the progress of IT. The effect on archaeological research is already visible in institutional terms: mathematical methods of classification are now part of most academic curricula, and a number of reputed scholars seem to regard formal methods as part of the necessary toolkit of archaeology 'as a science'. The real question, however, in the perspective of this conference, concerns the impact on the content of archaeological research. We might phrase it crudely as follows: can it be shown that our knowledge of past societies has improved, in quantitative or qualitative terms, as a result of the introduction of computer-based techniques of ordering the archaeological data upon which this knowledge is founded?

Answers differ according to whom you consult on this matter. My own feeling is that few scholars, if any, can grasp the full range of computer applications of that sort, throughout the world and in branches of archaeological research from Palaeolithic to modern times; any sweeping statement for archaeology as a whole, whether positive or negative, would therefore be questionable. There is, however, another way to approach the issue: rather than try to evaluate an overly large set of computer-based orderings of archaeological evidence and their interpretations, we may choose to focus our attention on the methodology, in order to draw out some common principles or postulates and assess *their* own value, irrespective of the context of application.

Let me first pass quickly over the case of sampling techniques, only to recall that they belong to the set of ordering methods under review in the broad sense proposed. Their severe limitations, both statistical and epistemological, are enough to deter us from expecting that our knowledge of the past will gain much strength from a more widespread use of such techniques through computerization.

Turning to classification, the common denominator which we are looking for can be found in the so-called heuristic strategy followed in most applications of mathematics and computers to the detection of formal structures in archaeology. The principle is well-known: given a set of objects described through a list of attributes, various configurations can be formed on the basis of mathematical expressions of intuitive concepts such as analogy, similarity, proximity, etc. The postulate is that the formal structures thus computed will suggest interpretations of one sort or other (historical, anthropological), that should eventually supersede the more traditional constructs by virtue of their mathematical merits alone. I have no quarrel with the principle: the amazing variety of statistical techniques grouped under the broad titles of 'data analysis' or 'analyse des correspondances' have amply demonstrated their ability to bring out a number of patterns designated in more or less naturalistic terms (trees, clouds, clusters, scales, etc.). But the postulate leaves me uneasy: why should such patterns be deemed *a priori* more 'interesting' or meaningful than those which we observe through other ways, unamenable to the aforesaid procedures? Further, why should we restrict the scope of formalization to the latter? Is it not conceivable that our intuitive or impressionistic groupings be open to *a posteriori* rationalizations no less formal than statistical procedures but based on calculi of another kind—grammars, automata, decision trees and the like?

Questions of that sort have been raised many times in the history of science, under different formulations, long before the progress of the computational paradigm happened to revive them with added force. Most of the classification constructs which have proved their worth in archaeology are the product of reasonings that owe nothing to mathematics nor even to the crudest variety of formal logic. This does not mean that they are not computable, in the guise of Turing machines; nor is it self-evident that statistical models of such constructs are preferable to their rationalizations in logical or logico-linguistic terms, as used, for instance, in AI programs. As a matter of fact, I tend to give more credit to the latter, because of a stubborn inability to believe in the virtues of the heuristic strategy in the research process. The impressionistic orders by which we live in archaeology should be regarded as so many *hypotheses*, in the same way as—or better still as a correlate, consequent, component of the interpretations which they are intended to support, as long as no empirical observations seem to contradict them. In this perspective, their formal roots in the database matter less than their cognitive offshoots. A similar viewpoint was once expressed apropos of statistical sampling itself: 'there is little doubt that purposive selection is preferable to sampling whenever selection is feasible, sufficient for one's research objectives and not wasteful' (Cowgill, in Mueller, 1975i).

Purposive selection: we have now reached a point where we can generalize the formula. We do not select only the sets or subsets of entities—artefacts, monuments, texts, ecofacts—upon which we intend to base our historical or anthropological constructs; we also choose to describe them in terms of certain features (properties, attributes) drawn from a much larger, in fact unbounded list. And we also select sensible orderings of the ones in terms of the others (entities according to features or features according to entities) for the purpose of assigning to each one of them a particular meaning, which is the ultimate goal of the whole exercise, from sampling to interpretation. The relation between the various components of such constructs—corpus, description, ordering (analogies, typologies, time series, etc.), interpretation—may be *presented* in either of two ways, bottom-up or top-down; this, of course, does not mean that we have actually *reasoned* according to the so-called empirico-inductive or hypothetico-deductive method alone while going from observations to theories. Only, once a symbolic construct has taken shape in our heads as a result of countless steps back and forth between the two, we have to phrase it in the form of a linear argument, which may then proceed from 'facts' to 'conclusions' (forward chaining) or from 'hypotheses' to 'facts' (backward chaining), with equal facility.

This approach to the methodological issues that have been with us for many decades in archaeology is regarded by most as a typical product of our computer age. It probably is; but one should be careful not to confuse the approach with the computer. Turing machines were conceived before electronic machines were built; and there are no 'logical' reasons why we should not have handled any of these above issues in the same pragmatic fashion prior to the advent of computers—or Turing machines themselves for that matter—as our colleagues in the natural sciences have done for quite some time (Lévy, 1987, plus any of the innumerable papers written by scientists or their philosophical exegetes on the structure of scientific theories).

Granted this reservation, I would submit that the major impact of the computer in archaeological research lies, or will eventually lie, in the perfusion of the so-called computational paradigm in our discipline—with or without computers. There are, of course, two well-established objections to that prognosis, the one technical, the other philosophical. The technical one, first: if the interpretive component is indeed the determinant factor in our reasoning processes, as suggested above, what do we do when we have to sample, describe and classify archaeological remains *in terra incognita*? Then, the philosophical objection: isn't this 'computational paradigm' a kind of Trojan horse loaded with dangerous (neo-)positivists, age-long enemies of the humanistic tradition? I shall try to answer both questions in the two following sections.

Interpretations

There are several ways in which it could be argued that computers have already had an impact upon the interpretation of archaeological remains.

First comes a rewording of the arguments that support the development of computer tools of the kind just discussed—databanks or classification programs—namely, that they help us to form and test our ideas about the meaning of our finds. I have already indicated the limitations, to me, of heuristic strategies in this rather primitive form; the tools of computer graphics, for instance, useful as they may be in their superb, more advanced versions, would be subject to similar reservations.

Another, more direct approach to computer-aided interpretation is through the concept of simulation. Archaeologists, as historians, study change, under any qualification (cultural, technological, societal, etc.); they have done so for many decades—rather successfully, in my view—using the intellectual means of their time, namely variables and values differentiated mostly in qualitative terms, and correlations formulated as interdependent propositions in natural discourse, with open-ended discussions on the essence of the dependency relation at work in each particular context.

Then came dynamic system modelling, and through it a strong inclination on the part of a 'new' brand of archaeologists to translate the natural logic of their not-so-new colleagues into computable terms, using quantified variables, numerical functions of change—continuous or discrete—and problem-solving techniques borrowed from mathematics or computer science (differential calculus, linear programming, etc.). The question which we have to raise here is the same as in the preceding sections: are we in a position to evaluate the contribution of such models to our understanding of human evolution or history in general?

Opinions would again differ according to which range of time and space, or which archaeological school one has in mind. To take but one example, prehistorians seem more prone than classical archaeologists to rely on simulation models for expressing and testing their interpretations of past phenomena. We can, however, follow in this case the same course as above, with respect to computer-based classification techniques, *i.e.* look for some common principles in the present methodology that may give us a hint of its potential utility in our discipline.

One such principle seems to be that the goodness-of-fit of computed to observed data is enough to establish the validity of the interpretive or explanatory theory that the model is intended to express. Objections to this belief have come from many sides, not least from the rank of mathematicians themselves: (i) the uniformities reproduced by the calculus may be the result of several processes that are masked by the coarser idealization of the model; (ii) the quantification of relationships adopted in the model often originates from observation domains that are not self-evidently 'analogous' to the domains of application; (iii) the parameters of formal systems are usually expressed as constants, while we have some reasons to believe that they change over time and space in human systems; (iv) although the language of catastrophe theory might seem to meet this obstacle, we are still left in the dark as to the effect which a given (set of) discontinuous shift(s) is likely to have on other constraints of the system in any concrete situation, etc.

None of these objections should be taken to mean that mathematics have no place in archaeological interpretations: after all, equations can usually be adjusted to fit any number of external conditions suggested by a growing body of experience. Only, we should be aware of the fact that, in saying this, we seem implicitly to admit that the major lesson of computing lies precisely in this drift towards 'local' models or theories, away from the general systems and universal laws which the 'new' archaeology had taken as its goal not so long ago.

A different computer-based approach to interpretation has recently emerged in archaeology, in the context of AI. The methodology in this case is associated with crude forms of logic rather than mathematics: the goal is to simulate or emulate the kind of argument used by archaeologists in natural discourse, either in the final presentation of interpretive constructs or in the actual process of theory-building, prior to publication. The computer tools are somewhat different according to which of those two situations is considered: inference engines in the former, intelligent conversational systems in the latter. In both cases, however, the major component is the 'knowledge base'; its function is to record the 'data' and 'rules of inference' used by 'experts' in a given 'field'. The inverted commas indicate words borrowed from the terminology of expert systems, with a meaning that is not necessarily quite the same as in the preceding sections of this paper. The concept of 'data', for instance, does not have the same extension as in the context of archaeological databanks; nor do the 'rules' of inference have the same status as the operations observed in archaeological argument when an author *A* derives a proposition or consequent *q* from a preceding set of propositions or premises *p*. I shall concentrate on those two points, because they provide us with answers to one of the two questions left open at the end of the preceding section: how do archaeologists behave, intellectually speaking, *in terra incognita*?

Let us imagine that an international team of archaeologists belonging to different 'cultures', whatever that may mean, has been entrusted with a survey of ancient sites and monuments in some remote part of the world about which nothing is known, except that human life was once present there. Man-made objects and structures are indeed found; but they are not readily comparable to the kind of objects and structures with which our experts are familiar. In other words, the cumulated expertise of the group is not enough, or rather not adequate to 'make sense' of the archaeological finds. Yet, it is expected from our experts that they should describe and classify them, for display purposes or others, even though they have no interpretation to offer. I need do no more than state the problem in those terms to convey the lack of solution, as a matter of principle, other than preserving the whole collection as it was found for the benefit of better equipped scholars. Failing which, our experts will inevitably have to draw upon their knowledge of material culture in general, ancient or modern, native or foreign, in order to come up with some proposal in their effort to salvage some piece of the human heritage, or their professional reputation. Thus, even in this case, the objects or phenomena selected and recorded as 'data' are but a reflection of our *past* experience as interpreters—professional or other.

A truism? Certainly, but its consequences do not seem to be universally clear. Although the same word is used, the 'data' that support scientific interpretations in the making have a distinct and totally different status from the data in information stores: they may have never been selected and recorded as such in the past. One of the virtues of the AI perspective in archaeology is that it forces us to give some thought to such issues, which have a direct bearing on the re-tooling of our discipline, both intellectually and technically. To make a long argument short,

I would submit that the databases evolved through the design and testing of expert systems should eventually enable us to prune the databanks associated with ISR systems, through a kind of self-reflexive learning process hitherto unfamiliar in archaeology.

A somewhat similar stand is suggested by the shift in the meaning or status of the word 'inference', as we go from natural discourse to artificial intelligence. Let us go back to author A and to his assumption that if premises p have been observed or established at any stage of the research process, then certain consequences q follow, the arguments that authorize this particular inference $p \longrightarrow q$ being more or less explicit in his presentation. The 'rule' component of a knowledge base is made up of many expressions $p \longrightarrow q$ of that sort, legitimated by the fact that 'experts' have used them at some time or other in their argumentations. There is, however, a considerable difference between the two situations. The inference carried out by author A is merely a discursive *operation* rooted in more or less established practices; while the same inference in an expert system is treated as a formal *rule*. Now, as we know, discursive practices are one thing, formal rules of reasoning another. An interesting aspect of computer aids to interpretation is that they inevitably bring out that very difference, in the form of ambiguous formulas of the type:

'IF p THEN EITHER $q1$ OR $q2$ ... OR qn'

In other words, the systematic recording of the 'more or less established' discursive practices shows that there are very few, if any, formal rules of reasoning proper to our discipline. The normal situation—at least in a statistical sense—is the one described above, where at any point p in the course of interpretation we are offered a variety of possible paths leading respectively to $q1$, to $q2$ ... or to qn, on the basis of past evidence in verbal behaviour.

Now, what are we supposed to do *then*? Leave it to the user of an intelligent conversational system to decide which path suits her or pleases him most? Or again try to prune the knowledge base, as suggested above with respect to 'data', by restricting the number of 'rules' to those which we can disambiguate, through an elicitation of the contexts, conditions or criteria of applicability?

The first course has many virtues: not only is it liberal, realistic, in harmony with the spirit and practice of interpretation in the humanities: it also happens to be magnificently easy. The second course, on the contrary, takes us back to our Trojan horse and the prospect of positivist infiltration into our stronghold. Most scholars today would probably resent and resist having any part in this. I share the same reluctance. Only, I think that we are, in this case, challenged by the new technology in a way that calls for a much stronger line of defence than we have been used to present in support of the specificity of the human sciences. This will be the subject of my conclusion.

Conclusion

You might first object that I have considered up to this point only three categories of computer applications, corresponding to three basic functions (information storage and retrieval, ordering or classification, interpretation): should we not broaden the scope of the survey before coming to any conclusions? There are, it is true, other categories of computer-based techniques to which archaeologists resort—e.g. wordprocessing, computer graphics, educational programs in various contexts (schools, museums, universities, etc.), etc. I am aware of this; leaving those applications out does not mean that I regard them as unworthy. Only, I have chosen to concentrate on the kind of issues that are more directly related to archaeological *research*, in keeping with my commitments in this conference and elsewhere. The degree of sophistication that goes into the design of increasingly powerful computer tools for editing manuscripts, visualizing objects, conducting classes, etc. is truly admirable; and I have nothing but praise for the wealth of uses to which they are being put in archaeology, especially in the UK, through the combined talents of computer experts and archaeologists often merged in the same persons. My concern, however, is not with the machinery, but with its observable effects on research, or more precisely with the progress of archaeological knowledge resulting from computer applications in the past years. The fact that a number of techniques have not been discussed in this paper is due to that narrow, perhaps short-sighted perspective: I have restricted my inquiry to those which have been applied widely enough, in time and space, to provide us with a proper empirical basis. (A similar argument holds for computer techniques that I seem to have forgotten, though they certainly fall within my own range, e.g. pattern recognition procedures, learning programs, etc.: they can indeed be regarded as combinations of ISR, ordering and interpretation processes, but at a level of complexity where only limited experiments have been carried out, with as yet no impact on archaeological knowledge proper).

Returning to the main thread of this paper, my conclusion would be that the development of IT in archaeology is likely to be one of the more powerful factors in the emergence or revival of fundamental issues that have in fact nothing to do with computers. The major one concerns the status of the symbolic constructs which we publish as scholarly commentaries on archaeological remains. Their reformulation in computable terms, motivated by an urge to take advantage of IT, brings out as clearly as we may wish the components of their architecture, i.e. the decisions which authors have taken, even if unconsciously, in selecting the materials and making sense of them through representation and processing techniques that are anything but 'natural', despite standing references to natural language and natural logic. Questions of decidability inevitably follow, as our computing exercises reveal the range of indeterminacy observed at every step of the calculus when we cumulate the knowledge bases of individual scholars.

Our common defence, at this stage, is that computability and decidability are out of place here: human phenomena are not of the same essence as physical phenomena, the human sciences are different from the natural sciences, we should not approach the human sciences with the same mental tools or requirements as the physical sciences, etc. I shall spare you the (post-)modern versions of this age-old duality; the interesting phenomenon, however, is the emergence of a Three-culture model (Lepenies, 1985), which is on the verge of giving birth to an embarrassing tetralogy (Figure 1). The trilogy is unstable enough: W. Lepenies has given us a convincing account of what he calls the *drift* of the human sciences towards Literature, as successive generations of specialists experience the ephemeral or local nature of established theories in their respective domains, with little sense of 'progress' from one to another (Lepenies, 1987). The anatomy of scholarly constructs which the computational paradigm helps to unveil brings out another puzzling feature—the *snag* in Figure 1—namely the fact that our reasoning processes in specialized fields do not differ much from those of everyday discourse, as practised by more or less enlightened laymen.

The two phenomena combined have interesting implications with respect to the status and fate of our theories in the humanities at large. This is probably not the place to discuss them. I only wish to submit that the most significant, if not always the most welcome consequences of computer-based techniques in archaeology, are likely to take the form of significant changes in the substance and form of presentation of our publications, according to the role which we assign to the computational paradigm in the build-up of scholarly constructs.

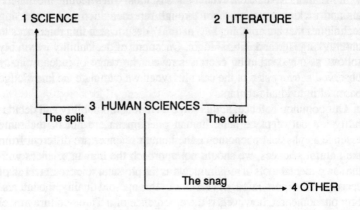

Figure 1: The status of academic discourse in the Third Culture (Lepenies, 1985) between Science and Literature, and its relation with other, non-academic discourse.

Substance, first: a growing number of archaeologists now regard it as part of their function to present, at the same time as a given theory about a set of observations, the factors that determine the scope of that theory, i.e. the 'domain' of its applicability. In other words, self-reflexivity tends to be more widespread, if not popular, to a point and in terms hitherto unknown. The reformulation of theories as computable constructs is one aspect of that trend; the most significant innovation, however, lies in the kind of issues that are bound to follow, whether we raise them in the course and apropos of that very process, or only discover them *a posteriori* as we experience the non-transportability of the knowledge bases associated with our constructs. The only way to 'save' the latter then consists in specifying the context in which we take them to be valid. 'Context' should here be understood in a very broad sense, which includes such diverse elements as geo-chronological coordinates, ethnographical comparisons, systems of beliefs or creeds, reference to the consensus of an 'interpretive community' or 'discursive society', in

Michel Foucault's terminology), reliance upon commonsense, etc. The systematic quest for C-factors of that sort (notice the italics above, to which you may add conditions, complements, criteria, conventions, etc. to designate the object of the quest) is bound to affect the way we produce and consume archaeological theories: the attention will shift, I believe, from the various schools or paradigms which we used to regard as more 'valuable' or 'desirable' than others, at any given point in space and time, to the reasons we have to value or desire them after having elicited the C-factors implicit in their respective products.

You might, of course, object that this move towards relativism and its introspective ferment is a result of the 'cognitive revolution' which our species is supposed to be going through, rather than a consequence of the 'new information technology'. I would agree with this; only, the computational paradigm provides the necessary link between the two concepts.

As for the form of archaeological publications, changes are already visible in the directions taken here and there with respect to excavation archives: computerized records are increasingly regarded as an alternative to printed books in that case, on the assumption that the means of access will continue to improve, in technological, institutional and economic terms, to the point of superseding libraries. Since this trend is well-known, I would rather bring out another consequence of IT—or at least a consequence of my preceding argument—regarding the style of our written presentations in archaeology. Reformulating them in computable terms is not just an exercise in applied logic or epistemology; it has some predictable effects on discourse as well. The argument is simple enough: if a computable version of our prose expresses the whole architecture of our reasoning, from materials to data (representation) and from data to theories (or conversely: processing), then why not present this version, which is more compact and easier to consult than a traditional article or book? Having tried such reductions myself, as much on my own papers (e.g. Gardin, 1988) as on those of others, I can testify that they have considerable value. Most scholars reject them, however, on the strength of an enduring attachment to natural language and traditional discourse as the 'normal' vehicle of thought in the humanities. They certainly have a point; but so have we, on the computational side, when we underline the paradox of a situation in which we are trained and expected to line up myriads of words that will not be *read*, except by only very few of the specialists for whom they are intended. I doubt that this phenomenon can outlast us very long, as more and more scholars are becoming aware of it, as well as of the directions in which remedies are to be looked for, in an evolutionary perspective (Gardin, 1987).

References

Gardin, J.-C. (1987) **Expert Systems and Scholarly Publications**. The Fifth British Library Annual Research Lecture, 1986. London: The British Library.

Gardin, J.-C. (1988) Case study no 1: the relations between Greece and Central Asia in the Hellinistic period according to ceramic data. In **Artificial Intelligence and Expert Systems: Case Studies in the Knowledge Domain of Archaeology** by J.-C. Gardin et al., pp. 61-87. Chichester: Ellis Horwood.

Lepenies, W. (1985) **Die drei Kulturen**. München: Carl Hanser. English translation: **Between Literature and Science: The Rise of Sociology**. Paris: Cambridge University Press and Editions de la Maison des Sciences de l'Homme, 1988.

Lepenies, W. (1987) Sur la guerre des sciences et des belles-lettres à partir du 18e siécle. **M.S.H. Informations** (Maison des Sciences de l'Homme, Paris), 54, 8-17.

Lévy, P. (1987) Le paradigme du calcul. In **D'une science à l'autre: des concepts nomades**, edited by I. Stengers, pp. 88-118. Paris: Seuil.

Mueller, J.W. (1975) **Sampling in Archaeology**, (i) p.260. Tucson: The University of Arizona Press.

The Scholar and the Research Environment

The Scholar, Technology, The Research Community, and its Institutions

A.J. Meadows
Loughborough University of Technology

Introduction

How should the research community be defined for the purposes of this paper? If asked about their 'research community', scholars in the humanities might respond: (1) in a narrow sense, the community consists of themselves and their peers carrying out research on a particular specialized topic; (2) in a wider sense, it embraces all scholars in their subject field; (3) in the widest sense, it means all scholars in the humanities. At the same time, they might phrase their response in terms of institutions. The community within an institution, such as a university, comprises all its humanities-related departments and research centres, and maybe some of the library staff, too. Outside universities, there are all the individuals and groups which, together, form each of the learned societies. Perhaps the community should also include all the bodies that are essential for the health of its research, such as research libraries, scholarly publishers and grant-giving agencies. Here, a middling definition of community will be used that covers all scholars and all the academic institutions that house them, together with the learned societies to which they belong, and the libraries they use.

The role of institutions

If technology is to have an impact on research, it must obviously be readily available to the scholar. This is one of the basic roles of the scholar's institution. The need to use technology may arise from pressures within the institution (e.g. for teaching, or as a substitute for a secretary), or from outside. If the pressure is internal, there is at least a fair chance that appropriate technology will be made available. This is not necessarily so with external pressure. For example, I have just contributed a chapter to a multi-author work which asks for input from a machine different from those possessed either by myself or my secretary. Fortunately, our department does have the equipment to get round this difficulty. As this illustrates, scholars today must have access to a range of information technology, which is usually only feasible within an institutional environment. It is true that individual researchers increasingly have their own micro at home but this may well be incompatible with equipment elsewhere (indeed, IBM compatibles are not necessarily compatible with each other). Moreover, hardware and software become outdated more rapidly than the individual pocket can accommodate: nor can the individual easily keep up with the changes in standards, maintenance costs, and so on. Hence, although simple wordprocessing at home may serve humanities scholars very well, they almost always need the backup provided by an institutional base, if they are to interact with the world at large.

The main problem for scholars in the humanities is that their institutions have typically funded humanities research at a relatively low level. At such a level, even micros are expensive: with most academic budgets currently tight, it has proved quite difficult to justify major expenditure on departmental computing facilities for research. This is partly offset by the increasing value of central facilities to humanities researchers. In most academic institutions, every department has a right to make its voice heard regarding central computing facilities. In recent years, humanities departments have increasingly pressed their requirements, where necessary at the expense of the specialist requirements of scientists or engineers, with the result that many institutions have moved to more flexible distributed systems, of special value to humanities scholars, instead of the 'number-crunchers' of a few years ago.

Teaching and training

Much of the internal pressure for introducing computers in the humanities has actually been for teaching purposes rather than for research. Computer-aided teaching is increasingly easy to justify, as the potential impact of computers on humanities teaching becomes more and more evident. In addition, funding for teaching equipment may be more readily available than funding for research equipment. An example of this is provided in the UK by the CTI (Computers in Teaching Initiative) Centres which have recently been established by the Computer Board. These cover most academic subjects, including all the main fields in the humanities, and are intended to act as foci for improving computer-aided teaching. (At the moment, best practice in such teaching is probably still found at leading centres in the USA, although differences between an average institution in the UK and the USA may not be so large.) The important factor for humanities researchers is that equipment purchased for teaching can also be used for research, especially during vacations (when much humanities research is, in any case, done). Partly as a result of this teaching emphasis, the material basis for using computers in humanities research during the 1990s should become quite well-founded.

One point which needs stressing is the effect of the rapid rate of change on all things connected with computing. Many humanities researchers have had to come to terms with a range of new technology in a short space of time. Their interest is not in the technology as such, but in what it can do. Yet the rapid change means that they must be constantly revising their technological knowledge. It is true that systems are becoming easier to use. Nevertheless, there is a continuing need both for training and for expert advice. Academic institutions do provide training for humanities scholars, either in-house, or as a shared arrangement between different institutions. An increasing number of sessions are now being organized for a wider audience by researchers themselves—for example, via society meetings.

In a sense, we are in a transition stage, because tomorrow's researchers are being introduced to computing now in their courses. It is today's scholars who are having to adapt most radically to the change. However, the difference is not as clear-cut as this would suggest. In the first place, the constant change of technology may mean that what we teach now will be of little use in twenty years' time. Thus, humanities scholars often have excellent keyboarding skills, which helps their transition to computing. In twenty years, voice input may have become sufficiently common that such skills lose their importance. In the second place, the academic institutions with the highest research prestige—which makes them the likeliest producers of the next generation of scholars—are not necessarily the most advanced in teaching applications of information technology.

If training represents a problem, the proper provision of expert advice is an even greater one. The greatest deterrent humanities scholars face in using information technology is the incidence of low-level system failures, or errors. These can be easily corrected—so long as expert advice is readily available. Unfortunately, humanities departments, unlike science departments, can rarely afford to employ computing staff to provide such advice. Some departments have self-trained academic staff who can help; but not only is this an inefficient way of using their time, beyond that they are often to be found among younger, temporary staff where turnover is high. Humanities departments must therefore often rely on help from experts in the institution's computer centre. Although helpful on longer-term questions, such computer staff are rarely able to give the immediate diagnosis that is needed if staff motivation is to be retained. Independent research centres can suffer even more in this respect. Many centres in the humanities are small: even if sufficiently well-funded to acquire adequate hardware and software, they are likely to be short of expert advice on the spot. This is one aspect of a wider question—the lack of suitable infrastructure. Many humanities departments and centres simply do not have the means to develop the applications of information technology to their subjects in a systematic way. Rather, their development is *ad hoc*.

Scholars as authors

Provision of resources to humanities scholars is one side of an equation: the other is, to what extent do the scholars wish to make use of such resources? It may be instructive to quote some of the characteristics that productive writers in psychology have been found to possess according to a recent survey (Hartley and Branthwaite, 1989). They:

- set the goals and targets of writing for themselves
- produce text by wordprocessing (either by themselves, or with secretarial assistance)

- write mainly at home
- rarely consult their colleagues or students about what they are writing
- rarely collaborate with other colleagues (but, if they do, work separately and then put the parts together).

Psychologists frequently carry out research as a member of a group, yet, even so, often write alone. Humanities researchers often carry out their research alone, as well as writing in equal isolation. Given that, in what sense can the scholarly community as a whole mediate, or influence the role of information technology on researchers? One answer—to be returned to later—is that technology may influence research in such a way as to encourage group participation. More immediately, even isolated researchers are involved in the community when they submit their work for publication, and this—as with psychologists—increasingly involves new technology.

The expectation that input will be available in machine-readable form has grown rapidly amongst book publishers in recent years. This is less true of journal publishers but, since humanities scholars publish a greater proportion of their research in books than other researchers, this is less important for them. Consequently, not only has wordprocessing become commonplace in the humanities, so has the need to work more closely with publishers in handling the machine-readable output. Even for journals, wordprocessing can also be used to produce camera-ready copy; this, too, has become a commonplace of humanities publishing (sometimes permitting the publication of work that would otherwise be financially non-viable). Since good mechanical printers are still moderately expensive, production of adequate camera-ready copy usually requires access to institutional facilities. Camera-ready copy for journals can raise some questions for the research community. For example, what happens to authors from developing countries, who do not have access to the necessary technology? So far, at least, this has not become a serious problem—publishers will prepare manuscripts in-house—but the question of cost differentials may become more important as journal profit margins are squeezed. Here, and elsewhere, we must put a query against information technology. Can its use make scholarship less international?

One area of rapid change has been the acceptability of wordprocessed material. Ten years ago, few senior scholars in the humanities regarded the printouts of wordprocessed material as suitable for anything except the wastepaper basket. Now the quality of material that can be obtained from a relatively cheap desktop publishing facility is such that many humanities scholars are considering the possibility of self-publication. Although DTP may be used on an individual basis, the interest so far, has been from groups working within similar, or related research areas. The most popular DTP products have been newsletters, or other relatively ephemeral material (e.g. posters, handouts). One area that is only beginning to be exploited is the use of desktop publishing for the rapid production of conference proceedings, including the inclusion of late alterations and discussion.

Software and data

At a more subterranean level, the provision and circulation of software— typically developed by individual enthusiasts and made available to their peers free of charge—has been fundamental to the advance of computing techniques in humanities research. Nowadays, commercially produced software is becoming increasingly useful for research, although only in areas, such as genealogy, where a wider market can be discerned. Fortunately, teaching software, for which better sales are likely, can often be used in research. An obvious example is provided by the various statistical packages that can be deployed to analyze data.

In addition, datasets in machine-readable form are becoming widely available—some from individual researchers or groups, some commercially, and a considerable number from government or other official sources. The amount of data available is such that the provision of central data archives has become an unavoidable requirement for efficient storage and retrieval. The social scientists went down this road some time ago: as witness, for example, the long-established ESRC Data Archive in the UK. This may perhaps be contrasted not too unfairly with the exploration of a Historical Data Archive for the UK which has only got under way recently. Even for social scientists, however, the position is not perfect. According to a recent survey, for example, the Inter-University Consortium for Political and Social Research (ICPSR) in the USA only covers a proportion of the machine-readable datasets which are of interest to its users, despite major efforts (Gould and Handler, 1989). Along with datasets, full-text databases are growing in number and importance. As with datasets, the expansion has been such that central archiving is now becoming essential. An example in the UK is the archive at Oxford University, which stores text in a wide range of languages. In return for the assistance that they provide to users, a copy of any text rendered in machine-readable form must be deposited by the user, so that it is available to other scholars.

Group research

This example underlines one of the advantages of community action, as against action by the individual researcher. Input of information to computer systems is the bottleneck in much technology-based humanities research. Progress can be made much more rapidly if the inputting load is spread, and the resultant jointly-created data made easily available to all those involved. Hence, groups—either *ad hoc*, or forming part of an institution such as a society—have become a common way of creating extensive data files. One of the examples often quoted of such community action is the successful Thesaurus Linguae Graecae project. In some instances, the material consists of the original papers of a particular individual or group, which may not otherwise be readily available to researchers. In others, it can be published material which is, for some reason, difficult for scholars to access. (In some ways, such files have a rather similar purpose to the older use of microform copies.)

The move towards using electronic products often requires the activities of a group, with its members encompassing a range of skills. Some research areas are now well-established—automated concordance and dictionary production, for example. In these, the already existing experience of humanities scholars is often all that is needed for efficient despatch of a new research project. Such 'established' areas of research competence are, for example, reflected in a conference to be held in the UK in 1991. It is aimed at humanities scholars from all over the world who are involved in developing computerized dictionaries of Greek and Latin, along with those who are concerned with automated lemmatizers, parsers, translation aids, and intelligent tutors.

The mixture of research and teaching aids implied by the 'intelligent tutors' is typical of humanities scholarship: the two activities can interact in terms of software, datasets, etc., in a way that is rare in the sciences. Another example is provided by the growth of multimedia input and output. Work on handling socio-economic statistics via the graphics of cartographic interfaces can be applied either for research purposes, or to create student exercises. The ability to cross-refer the data is equally valuable in either context.

Much of the software used in research has required the input of skills from outside the humanities profession (most obviously on the computing side). Progression into new applications typically entails calling on outside expertise, even though humanities researchers are themselves becoming increasingly knowledgeable. To some extent, this position is being changed by the availability of sophisticated software from commercial sources (although its price may create problems for the average humanities researcher). For the future, it can be expected that scholars in the humanities who are following well-trodden paths (from the viewpoint of methodology and technology) will find all the help they need within their community, but innovation will still require assistance from a wider grouping.

Networking

Information technology is broadening the size of the community available for consultation via the use of electronic networks. At the simplest level (in terms of user skills), fax has become an excellent way of exchanging information internationally, not least because it can be used to transmit diagrams as well as text. The problem with fax is twofold—cost and availability. For a small humanities department, extensive use of fax may be ruled out purely on grounds of money. In any case, the fax machine may be so inconveniently situated relative to the department that its use becomes too time-consuming. Email is usually less limited by cost (due to the existence of subsidized networks), but suffers even more from the problem of siting. The information here has to be keyed in directly (whereas fax can be handwritten or typed elsewhere and then sent to a remotely sited machine). There is extensive evidence to show that regular use of Email requires researchers to have terminals on their desks. Until humanities departments can all afford this, Email will not produce its maximum effect (although its use is already on the increase).

Bulletin boards are usually referred to at less frequent intervals than Email, so the need for an immediately available terminal is less important. Researchers are willing to see its use as the equivalent of a library visit. Correspondingly, bulletin boards have become a rapidly growing area of electronic communication in the humanities community. An example of the types of interaction involved is provided by HUMBUL (the Humanities Bulletin Board) in the UK, which has been run for some years by the Office for Humanities Communication. Its contents are intended not only to facilitate research indirectly—by disseminating information about conferences, etc.—but also directly, for example, by running a 'notes and queries' section. Experience with HUMBUL underlines an important point about electronic communication: it typically supplements print-on-paper communication, rather than replaces it. In this instance, a *Humanities Communication Newsletter* is run in parallel with HUMBUL. It was clear from the start that, although some material is suitable for publication both by the bulletin board and the newsletter, much is better displayed via one of these outlets only. For example, longer articles are not suitable for a bulletin board, whilst information that requires reasonably speedy dissemination is not suitable for the newsletter.

Which outlet—electronic or hard copy—is better for a particular type of communication depends not only on the nature of the information involved, but also on the answers to a variety of socio-economic questions. For example, online journals containing new research articles encounter several such problems—from acceptability by one's peers of the medium as a purveyor of research to the difficulty of international electronic distribution—which may well leave them as of marginal interest for a number of years to come. In a rather different vein, computer conferencing is now relatively straightforward in terms of technology but, for a range of reasons, many researchers are not very interested in using it. Consequently, it is currently supported by enthusiasts, but still ignored by many.

Information retrieval

The longest established use of information technology in the humanities is online retrieval, mainly of bibliographic data. This might seem an obvious area where the humanities community should make use of a shared store of centralized information. In fact, online bibliographic retrieval has not proved as popular as might have been expected (Morton and Price, 1986). One problem is the availability of relevant databases. Those of direct interest to humanities scholars are comparatively few: provision is best in areas overlapping the social sciences. Where relevant databases are provided—for example, by the Modern Language Association in the United States—uptake of the service by researchers in the humanities noticeably improves. Nevertheless, as a recent Norwegian survey has underlined, there is still only a limited enthusiasm for such bibliographic databases amongst researchers (Lönnqvist, 1988).

For many researchers, however, it is not the generally available bibliographic databases that concern them, but the personal databases that they put together themselves, often on their own micros. Increasingly, the question is whether the innumerable, scattered personal databases now in existence can, in some way, be made more widely available, since there is much duplication of effort at present. Here is a need for an initiative that must clearly be community-based. The question is how to go about it, given not only the difficulty of finding out what exists, but also the variety of the hardware and software used in handling and storing the information.

Now that CD-ROM mastering is becoming rapidly cheaper, it may be that locally held databases will prove more popular than online access to remote hosts. CD-ROM has an immediacy that online access does not, since the latter is often delegated to trained searchers in the library. At the moment, a number of questions remain. The cost of CD-ROMs plus equipment is such that most material will be held centrally by the institution's library. Will this affect use? What humanities material will it be financially feasible to put on disc? Optical discs, in general, unlike online access, provide an excellent way of providing graphics, as well as text, in electronic form. Does this mean that databases on disc will be of particular value to graphics-based subjects (such as history of art)? There is already some evidence to suppose that researchers are happier with local access to CD-ROM than with remote access to online databases; so humanities scholars may change their attitude to such information retrieval and its value in the coming decade.

Research libraries

The electronic development of interest to humanities scholars which is evolving most rapidly at present relates to library catalogues. The growth of online public access catalogues (OPACs) has affected researchers in a number of ways. When actually in the library, it allows for more efficient identification of holdings; but it also permits such access to each department via a local area network to each department, so helping to make visits to the library more fruitful. A third of US scholars questioned in 1985 said that computerized catalogues had enhanced access for them (Morton and Price, 1986). Yet the full value of OPACs has yet to be realized, via a transition from local to wide area networks. The ability to examine the holdings of major research libraries elsewhere, whilst sitting at one's own desk, can obviously be a major time-saver. As systems become more sophisticated, it should be possible to go further—for example, to reserve a particular volume online at a library prior to a visit there.

The main bottleneck slowing down the fulfilment of this vision is, once again, the transformation of printed information into electronic form. Many libraries now automatically input information on new acquisitions to their OPACs. This is fine for areas such as science, where information dates rapidly, so that all the important items will have been captured into the OPAC within (say) ten years. Humanities scholars, on the contrary, are often interested in older material: indeed, they are often chasing this when they visit libraries other than at their home institution. This means that there is a massive problem of retrospective conversion for research libraries in the humanities. One problem is that attempts to decide which titles might be selectively entered into the OPAC have typically foundered on disagreements between the scholars themselves on what is, and what is not, important material. Hence, a policy of blanket coverage tends to be the most easily supportable. So far, most automated methods of inputting information (such as optical character recognition) have proved to be ultimately as time-consuming as manual keyboarding. Cooperation between those libraries with major research holdings in the humanities seems the only way forward. That scholars are genuinely interested in having older material catalogued electronically is suggested by the attention they have paid to the electronic version of the *Eighteenth-Century Short Title Catalogue*.

The acceptance of information technology

Scholarly use of information technology has naturally grown in a haphazard manner—sometimes due to individual initiative, sometimes institutional. What is evident as the field matures is that it is creating its own institutions. The application of computers was seen, at least initially, as a distinctive activity, and led correspondingly to the creation of new research centres. The *Humanities Computing Yearbook* lists some hundred of these in North America and Western Europe. Group interest in applications of information technology sometimes appeared under the aegis of an existing learned society. More often, it was started as a fringe activity by enthusiasts. Consequently, the expanding wave of computer-based research has led to the appearance of new societies and new publications. But as applications become more widespread, so existing societies and publications are adjusting to accept them. The degree of acceptance still depends on research orientation. Parts of linguistics and philosophy, for example, interact so obviously with automated handling of information that practitioners in these areas have accepted computer-based research for some time, not only as a provider of aids to research, but as a tool in the research process itself. Other areas—such as general literary or art criticism—accept the technology as an aid, but still have to agree on its usefulness as part of the research process.

One thing that has become clearer is that humanities researchers are perfectly capable of becoming skilled users of information technology, if their motivation is strong enough. Indeed, several significant developments in information technology nowadays are into areas where input from humanities specialists has become increasingly useful. Consequently, major firms in the computing industry have been recruiting for some time people with backgrounds in disciplines such as classics, philosophy, linguistics or, now, geography. This convergence of interests raises a query regarding trends in humanities research itself. Is the existence of appropriate technology now affecting in a significant way which areas of research are chosen for exploration? From the viewpoint of the research community, a re-orientation towards computer-based research has a number of long-term implications—from funding to methodology.

The final question in considering the impact of information technology on humanities research relates to recognition by the community. Are researchers who make major use of such technology receiving appropriate recognition? The question is particularly difficult to answer because many applications are still new, and have often been introduced by younger researchers who will, in any case, require time to achieve full recognition. However, in research areas, such as demography, which have been aided by information technology, but preceded it, recognition has already been forthcoming. What seems likely is that assessment of research may have to change somewhat as computer-based research expands. A major application of information technology usually requires the award of a sizeable research grant. The pursuit of such grants is currently encouraged by the institutional ethos (if not necessarily by that of individual researchers). Being major, the project is likely to require the services of a research group, rather than a single individual. There may be the potential here for something like the 'big science, little science' split that has affected science to manifest itself in the humanities. Hence, the increasing use of information technology may have two opposite outcomes in humanities scholarship. On the one hand, it may emphasize the importance of group research, on the other, it may act to fragment the existing humanities research community further into big well-financed groups and small groups or individuals who have to work within a more limited range of research opportunities.

References

Gould, C. and Handler, M. (1989) **Information Needs in the Social Sciences: An Assessment**. Palo Alto: Research Libraries Group.

Hartley, J. and Branthwaite, A. (1989) The psychologist as wordsmith: a questionnaire study of the writing strategies of productive British psychologists. **Higher Education**, 18, 423-452.

Lönnqvist, H. (1988) **Humanister soker information eller "Motet med den litauiske skoputsaren"**. NORDINFO- publikation, 13. Esbo: NOR-DINFO.

Morton, H.C. and Price, A.J. (1986) The ACLS survey of scholars: views on publications, computers, libraries. **EDUCOM Bulletin**, 21, 8-21.

A National Information Infrastructure for Research and Scholarship

A.J. Forty

University of Stirling

Introduction

I have been asked to speak about the national dimension of the use of technology in research and scholarship in the humanities. Whilst recognizing that research in the humanities has different objectives, involves different methodologies and requires greatly different conceptual powers, I see a fascinating convergence with research in the social sciences, and indeed in the natural sciences, as far as the impact of information technology is concerned. Much of what I have to say in this paper is conditioned by my background in the physical sciences but my vision of a national information technology network provides an important space for the humanities.

Let me start to develop this view of convergence of research in the humanities and the sciences by referring to Figure 1. Here we see that, unlike the situation in the case of the humanities, there has been hitherto a divergence between teaching and research in the sciences.

It has been stated elsewhere in this Conference that the interplay between research and teaching occurs inevitably, and most naturally in the humanities. That is not to say that such interplay should not exist in other branches of learning but, particularly in the second half of the twentieth century, the gulf between creating knowledge and acquiring knowledge has widened in most other areas. In physics, for example, the prior need for mastery of the basic concepts of quantum mechanics and the skills needed to manipulate the mathematical equations restrict the creativity of the undergraduate in areas such as the fundamental structure of matter where the most exciting research is being done. Even the good postgraduate student usually becomes fully creative only at the postdoctoral stage. I believe this will change as computers and other information systems become more fully integrated into teaching. For example, the presentation of the calculus and the concept of wave-particle duality which underlies the quantum mechanical description of matter can now be done much more effectively on a computer screen than was ever possible by 'board and chalk'. The student can simulate highly complex phenomena by computational methods and engage in 'experiments' which otherwise would be quite impossible. Thus, through the emergence of computational science we can expect an increasing convergence of teaching and research in the sciences (see Figure 1). The computational approach is already recognized to be a powerful new method of scientific research, complementing the traditional approaches of experiment and mathematical analysis. The use of powerful computers to construct models of complex molecules and their biological interactions, to simulate the epitaxial growth of semiconductors or to model the oceans and the atmosphere, and the complex interaction between them, means that the study of these and many other important areas which are of great socioeconomic importance, previously intractable to study in the laboratory, is now possible.

Figure 1: The convergence of teaching and research and the use of information technology in the humanities and sciences.

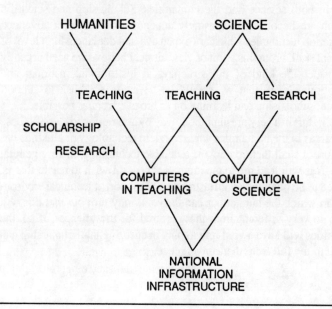

The congruence of teaching and research in the humanities and the impact of technology is leading to a different kind of convergence. Both teachers and students see information technology as a tool, or device to obtain information, to create text and analyze it, and to communicate and disseminate information. The tools required today range from simple wordprocessors and desktop publishing facilities to powerful, large-memory machines for text analysis. The needs of the arts and humanities are not going to be satisfied so easily in the future, especially when scholars begin to appreciate the opportunities available to them to exploit the computer for graphical display and the use of pictures and moving images. Such opportunities also pose a threat. The demands for more computationally intensive facilities and their lesser availability could lead to a divergence between teaching and scholarship. It could also lead to an intellectual divergence within the research community in the humanities if the technical 'know-how' as well as the availability of the necessary facilities becomes a dominant factor. The very rapid developments in this area in recent years makes an assessment such as that provided by this Conference vitally important. This brings me to the most important convergence in Figure 1. The use of computing and other forms of electronic technology in teaching and research is developing apace in both science and the humanities. Scholarship and scientific research are becoming increasingly dependent on the most advanced information techniques which are expensive and demand a high level of technical skill. From this point of view alone, I believe we need urgently to consider the kind of infrastructure, at institutional, national and international level, that we should be trying to establish to support research, scholarship and learning on as broad a front as possible.

I shall start in a very presumptuous way by attempting to identify those thrust areas in the humanities where modern technology of all kinds has a real use. I shall then review the available technology, in very general terms. This will lead me to the main conclusion I wish to reach; that is, we need to be planning an infrastructure of support, a technical environment, in which the humanities can thrive. It may turn out that this will not be so very different from that required for the sciences. If so, the humanities will have a vital role to play in ensuring that scholarship can benefit to the full from that convergence.

Technology in the humanities today

Figure 2 may be viewed as a map on which we can plot the course of contemporary developments in the humanities, and possible future developments as far as the use of information technology is concerned.

Figure 2: *A linear map of contemporary developments in information technology: this must be the basis of a national information infrastructure for research and scholarship.*

A NATIONAL INFORMATION INFRASTRUCTURE

WORDPROCESSING
ACCESS TO LIBRARY CATALOGUES
TEXT ANALYSIS

LAN   MAINFRAME PC'S

INTER-LIBRARY LOANS
CTI CENTRES
DATABASES
ELECTRONIC MAIL

JANET   WORKSTATIONS

COLLABORATIVE RESEARCH
DATABASES

JANET MKII   INTERACTIVE VIDEO
NETWORKS

LIBRARY RESOURCE SHARING
ELECTRONIC PUBLISHING
MOVING IMAGES

SUPERJANET   SUPERFAX

HUMANITIES WORKSHOPS

It is a reasonably safe assumption that the central feature of research in the humanities today is the use of the printed word. The use of image to convey ideas, and in communication generally, is growing and can be expected to develop dramatically as the appropriate technology becomes more readily available. However, most scholars need access to text to aquire information and use text to create and disseminate knowledge and understanding. Research and scholarship is therefore text-based and centred on the printed word. This gives us a clear definition of the current demand for technology in the humanities.

The wordprocessor based on the PC together with a portfolio of useful software has led to a quiet but nonetheless dramatic revolution in the means of preparation of text. The technological revolution goes well beyond simply replacing the typewriter by a more user-friendly tool. More exotic text-handling in the form of desktop publishing has opened up completely new dimensions for the textual presentation of ideas. The combination of the computer and modern image recording and reprographic technology has transformed the everyday communication between scholars as well as the more formal presentation such as those we experience in conferences such as this.

The use of computer-based technology is now accepted by the scholar in many other ways. For example, he has easier access to library catalogues. Databases of all kinds are becoming readily available for online use. Full-text databases are only just emerging but the use of electronic publishing technology will clearly accelerate developments in this direction.

However, these are all more or less simply aids to support the scholar in pursuit of knowledge in the traditional sense. The full impact of technology on scholarship is yet to be felt, although, as we are learning in this conference, there are already ways in which new methods of analysis and presentation of information are becoming available through the use of the computer. Concordances and text retrieval and the use of hypertext in literature studies are opening up exciting new approaches for both the researcher and the student. These are of course more demanding in terms of both machine and human resources. The preparation of text in machine-readable form and archiving require facilities which can only be provided on a centralized basis. This and the need to share the tasks in large- scale projects means that scholars in the humanities are now recognizing the need for a more cooperative approach. The Computers in Teaching Initiative Centre for Literature and

Linguistic Studies at the Oxford University Computing Centre (*Computers in Literature: Newsletter No.1*, January 1990) is a good example of what is happening at the level of teaching and student learning using the new medium of electronic communication. This brings with it a greater use of electronic mail, bulletin boards, and conferencing. The close interaction between research and teaching means that students, the scholars of tomorrow, too are beginning to realize the benefits of this kind of infrastructure.

The digital medium is also being exploited for graphical and image presentation of data. Digital maps have transformed the information base for geographers and geographical information systems (GIS) are powerful tools for research as well as in the practical applications of land use and planning. With the exception of studies of population dynamics, which require powerful supercomputers, this kind of research can be supported by equipment and software that is readily available and affordable on a cooperative basis.

We may conclude therefore that the technology needs of the humanities today range from the modest PC to fairly powerful mainframe computers and, in the more specialist applications, powerful workstations. Access to library catalogues, archiving and electronic communication means that networking is a vital part of the technology infrastructure.

The impact of new technology

The ability to create, analyze and transmit images of all kinds, and the availability of moving pictures will have a most dramatic effect on the approach to research and teaching in the humanities.

Even now, the ability to transmit facsimile images of text electronically has greatly assisted the communication between scholars. Inter-library loans can be expedited. It is possible, if British Telecom megastream facilities, and a suitably high budget, are available, to transmit high quality images so that high definition of text or half-tone illustrations can be disseminated. This has significant implications for the scholar who will need to use an inter-library loan scheme to share scarce materials in a situation where escalating costs and reducing budgets make this inevitable. Videoconferencing, using image and sound in real-time interactive mode is already used in business organizations. Interactive video networks, such as LIVENET which links the various components of the University of London, are beginning to emerge for academic purposes. These are being promoted as a means of sharing scarce resources in teaching but I believe the true value will be the new dimension that moving pictures can provide. Furthermore, electronic images can readily be recorded, archived, and accessed over a network.

In the sciences, where advanced research computing using supercomputers entails the handling of vast quantities of data which cannot be readily assimilated, greater emphasis is now being placed on visualization of the output. The supercomputer environment now being sought by scientists consists of advanced graphics facilities to convert data into assimilable form, a high speed network for data and image transmission to remote users and powerful local workstations for image manipulation in an interactive mode. Such an environment could of course be adapted for the creation, transmission and manipulation of text and pictures of all kinds.

A national infrastructure for computing and information services

All such developments of information technology depend on funding. In the humanities the rapidly increasing awareness of the opportunities offered by the new technology is being frustrated by restriction of resources, including skilled manpower as well as technical facilities. Even in the sciences facilities are restricted, particularly for advanced computational research. This means that the sharing of resources is inevitable. With the appropriate infrastructure, cooperative programmes should arise from this as an additional benefit. This has certainly been the experience elsewhere. Collaborative Computing Projects (CCPs) centred on the CRAY supercomputer have been very successfully established in a number of areas in the physical sciences.

The sharing of resources demands effective networking. The Joint Academic Network (JANET) established ten years ago by the Computer Board in the UK now plays an important role in providing access to centralized computing facilities at the Rutherford Appleton Laboratory (RAL), the University of London Computing Centre (ULCC) and the Manchester Computing Centre (MCC). There is also sharing of computing facilities on a regional basis. JANET is being used increasingly for general communication via electronic mail and for dissemination of information and materials for teaching between sites.

The existing network is now being enhanced by installing high speed (megastream) connections between main sites and very high speed local area networks based on fibre optics. The insistence on open systems means that a wide range of compatible machines can be connected to the network and access to local and central filestores and databases is available. The opportunities for researchers are therefore very extensive. The potential of this for workers in the humanities is being recognized by most universities who are now placing an increasing emphasis on distributing facilities via local area networks (LANs). From workstations in offices and classrooms staff and students have access to library catalogues and databases as well as computing power. Some universities have used this development to integrate libraries and computing in a comprehensive information service. The benefits include a more coherent planning of information services and easier access to data of all kinds. The transition to fibre optic technology through JANET mkII should mean that access to images and possibly video material will be available on a campus-wide basis.

The Computer Board, soon to become the Information Services Committee of the Universities Funding Council, has submitted a proposal to the UK Government for funds to instal SUPERJANET. This will be a fibre optic national network which will provide a very fast link between universities and colleges which by then will have converted their LANs. The initial stimulus for this is the need to provide high bandwidth connections between remote users and centralized supercomputers as part of the supercomputing environment referred to earlier. However, SUPERJANET will open up opportunities for communication and resource-sharing of all kinds. Access to library materials from remote images by fax over the high speed network, at low cost, will make the sharing of special library collections more realistic. Similar developments in the United States and in continental Europe should provide similar opportunities for the international research community.

A national or international community of scholars needs more than the hardware of such a network. The infrastructure must include national coordination of software, planned development of databases and, most important of all, a recognition of the need for technical staff to assist scholars and researchers in extracting full benefit from the facilities available to them. My vision of a national infrastructure for the support of research and scholarship in the humanities is therefore one in which collaboration and sharing of resources are promoted and encouraged by a high speed communication network linking universities, libraries and other information sources. The realization of this will depend as much on the willingness of scholars to collaborate as the preparedness of the funding agencies to provide.

Another Machine in the Garden: Information Technologies and Training the Research Scholar

John Howe

University of Minnesota

A host of rapidly developing information technologies, fashioned from the explosive synergism between computers and telecommunications, is rapidly reshaping the information environment and the processes of scholarship. My paper carries the subtitle, 'Information Technologies and Training the Research Scholar', which I understand to centre on the implications of the continuing revolution in information technologies for the education of graduate students in the humanities as they enter the academy. When I first began preparing this paper the topic seemed reasonably compact. As I thought about it, however, the boundaries quickly dissolved for I realized that if graduate students are to function effectively in the scholarly and information worlds of the future, even the near term future, they will need to be well informed about a whole host of ways in which computer based technology, information science, and humanistic scholarship interact. The more I thought, the more inclusive my agenda became. In the end, I have cast my net broadly across an array of informational and technological issues that aspiring humanists need to consider, while focusing my comments on what seem to me the issues of most compelling interest and importance.

I want first to offer some general observations on the evolving relationship between the humanities and information technology. Building on those observations, I then want to comment more specifically on the consequences of computing and telecommunications for how humanists write, for patterns of scholarly communication, for what librarians call bibliographic access, and for the ways in which humanists design and execute their research. I want, finally, to suggest some general implications of modern information technologies for the conduct of humanistic scholarship. Through it all my guiding concern will be the needs, not of the long experienced humanist, but of the novice just entering the profession and how those needs might shape graduate training programmes for the scholars of tomorrow.

First, some general observations about the intersections of humanistic scholarship and new information technologies. From the perspectives of both the research scholar and the academic librarian, it is clear that computerized information systems, whether dedicated to information access or the conduct of research, have affected scholarly inquiry in the humanities less dramatically, certainly less completely than in the physical and biological sciences, or in certain areas of the social sciences as well.[17] Computer technologies are clearly reshaping the ways in which countless humanists do their work. That is evident from the papers presented at this conference or a quick perusal of a journal such as *Computers and the Humanities*. Still, humanistic inquiry has not been as powerfully influenced by information technology as have scholarly investigation and discourse in other fields. There are several reasons for this: the much stronger mathematical and quantitative orientation of scientific and technical fields of knowledge; the existence of national libraries, such as the National Library of Medicine in the United States, that serve as organizing agencies for computerized information systems; the distinctive publishing conventions of the natural and biological sciences, especially their strong dependence on journal literature rather than book monographs; the equally distinctive patterns of scholarly communication in the sciences, for example the greater dependence on group research, national and international collaboration, and the steady exchange of working papers and other forms of pre-published materials; and the relatively large scale funding support that research scientists command. Each of these scholarly conventions places a premium on informational and research capabilities that only sophisticated computer technology can provide.

The physical and biological sciences, moveover, are inherently technology intensive—as well as technology expensive. The set up costs for equipment required by young laboratory scientists in chemistry, physics, and biology run easily into the hundreds of thousands of dollars. In addition, the natural sciences have intimate, reciprocal ties with engineering programmes. 'Technology transfer' is the label we give to the

---

17. See the recent report titled **Information Technology and the Conduct of Research** (Washington, 1989), sponsored by the National Academies of Science and Engineering.

practice of drawing practical applications out of basic scientific knowledge. We see its results in the burgeoning products of biotechnology, electronics, and space exploration.

Humanistic inquiry, by contrast, is neither technology oriented nor technology driven. Our 'laboratory' is still the library; our 'equipment', books and journals; our subject matter, language, literature, and artistic artefacts; and our dominant focus the study of human culture, whether considered as heritage to be studied and preserved or as the contested product of social discourse. In addition, as even a cursory review of *PMLA*, the *American Historical Review*, and other scholarly journals attests, humanistic inquiry remains for the most part non-quantitative, given more to textual analysis, narrative development or cultural theory construction than to quantitative analysis or the kind of empirically based theory testing that characterizes the natural and some areas of the social sciences.[18]

To the extent that humanistic inquiry is theory driven, moreover, most theoretical structures—whether deconstructionist, feminist, psychoanalytic, marxist, or otherwise—point away from quantitative analysis and draw instead on philosophical, linguistic, aesthetic, literary or historical modes of explanation.[19] To be sure, computational linguistics as well as a variety of social and political histories combine empirical research with quantitatively driven theory testing, but when they do they veer consciously toward the social sciences and away from the humanistic mainstream. With social and political agendas ascendant in much humanistic discourse these days and with the 'truth' of mathematically based empirical science no longer privileged, indeed vigorously contested, most humanistic scholarship is neither conceptually nor methodologically wedded to the machine.

That being said, the connections between humanistic inquiry and computer technologies are important and filled with significance, especially when one looks beyond the present state of things into the rapidly changing future, a future that today's graduate students will at once inherit and help to define. As information technologies continue to unfold

---

18. W. van Peer, 'Quantitative studies of literature; a critique and an outlook'. Computers and the Humanities, 23 (1989(301-307, examines the conceptual limitations of much mathematical analysis in the humanities.
19. In papers delivered at this conference, Professors J. Hillis Miller and George Landow argue that there is a unique fit between the technical capabilities of hypertext systems and the analytical approaches of much recent cultural theory, especially ideas of decentering, intertextuality, and anti-hierarchical texts.

and modes of humanistic scholarship evolve in the years ahead, scholars will continue to search out ways in which the machine can facilitate their work, especially younger scholars who will bring to the academy not only higher degrees of computer literacy, but bolder assumptions about computer applications in the work that they do. The relentless development of computer technologies and the equally relentless logic of actuarial tables together guarantee that humanistic scholarship and technology will continue to converge.

With those comments as preface, what can be said about specific information technologies and the training of young scholars in the humanities? I want to organize my comments around a brief typology or hierarchy of ways, from simplest and most self-evident to more complex and problematic, in which computer based technologies and humanistic inquiry intersect. Each needs to be addressed, more or less explicitly, in the graduate training we provide, if the graduate students of today are to function effectively as scholars in the technology-rich academic environment of tomorrow.

At the lower end of the hierarchy lie the relatively straightforward functions of wordprocessing provided by stand-alone or locally networked personal computers. Though the technical requirements of WordStar or WordPerfect, Microsoft Word or MacWrite may initially prove daunting to the novice, wordprocessing itself, even with its most extravagant display capabilities, is, with two possible exceptions, nonproblematic. The first exception is its devilish, geometric acceleration of the words that we produce, words that our libraries must struggle to acquire and that we, alas, are expected to read! If ever a blessing threatens, Midas-like, to become a curse, it is the greater technological facility with which we write. Whether personal or professional discipline can clamp down even partially on this compositional Pandora's Box, I have my doubts.

The second caveat involves the long term and still very unclear consequences of electronically assisted composition, not just for the speed with which we write but for how we write as well.[20] Might the increasingly sophisticated design capabilities of wordprocessing software strengthen manuscript appearance at the expense of substance?

---

20. Wayne Danielson, 'The writer and the computer'. **Computers and the Humanities**, 19 (1985) 85-88 discusses some of these issues.

Could more advanced and widely available compositional aids produce greater homogeneity of style? More troublesome, will the accelerated pace of research and composition result in shorter, less considered, and more transient publications? As the tempo of scholarly exchange increases, will scholars be as willing to undertake long-term projects of the sort that have historically anchored humanistic scholarship? Whatever the prospects, wordprocessing has become an essential support of the scholarship we do and our students need to know how to reap its benefits.

Second and more problematic, our students need assistance in learning about the myriad ways in which information technologies shape channels of scholarly communication, both informal channels of personal networking and the more formal processes of scholarly publication. Not all of us are yet connected into Bitnet, Arpanet, Internet or any of the other communications networks that now girdle the globe, but many of us are and more of us are certain to be. Not only do our younger colleagues need to know how to utilize these telecommunications systems, they need to ponder as well the implications of virtually instantaneous electronic communication across space. The prospects are exhilarating, for the free and unfettered exchange of knowledge is a guiding principle of scholarly life. And yet cautions are in order; for example, the cost implications for our universities of supporting unlimited, on-demand network access as well as the social and ethical implication of this new, technological discriminator between academic haves and have nots, between those who are privileged to communicate via these far flung channels of information exchange and those who are not.

The capacity to communicate easily and continuously from personal workstations across vast distances is likely to have other implications. Think, for example, of the solitariness with which humanists have traditionally done their work. As easy and cost efficient communication becomes a reality, will humanists move toward more collaborative research as their science colleagues have done? If so, what will be the implications for the research agendas that humanists pursue? Individuals will deal with these expanding networks of professional communication differently depending on subject area, the adequacy of traditional communication patterns, and even personal temperament. As younger colleagues head into the academy, however, they need to anticipate the future communication environment within which they will operate so they can make informed decisions about how they can best utilize it for their own purposes.

Computer applications also promise to alter the practices of scholarly publication. The fact that print publication is increasingly computer driven is already changing the ways in which authors, editors and the publishers of scholarly material interact. Some publishers, mostly as yet in the sciences, now allow, a few even require that manuscripts be submitted electronically via floppy disc. The day is perhaps not far distant when editorial processes such as the review of manuscripts and the ongoing dialogue between author and editor will be handled entirely online. Just as we have for years tutored our students on the folkways of traditional publication, so are we obligated to ready them for new publishing conventions.

Then there is the growing practice of electronic publication. Already widespread in areas of the natural sciences, law, and library reference materials, electronic publication is certain to become more common in the humanities. How rapidly it expands will depend on relative cost; resolving problems of user access, copyright and royalties; and dealing with long established readerly habits. Whether or not electronic publication becomes an irresistible wave of the future, it is certain to increase in importance. As it does, it will force changes in the ways scholars prepare their manuscripts and see them into 'print', including the peer review process by which scholarly standards have been maintained and common intellectual agendas given shape.

The emergence of so-called 'desktop' publishing, made possible by ever more powerful personal computers and ever more elegant software, is challenging long-held assumptions about what scholarly publishing entails. As some forms of publication become increasingly decentralized, the boundaries between refereed and non-refereed publications threaten to dissolve and scholarly oversight of the publishing process becomes less secure. Even more than those of us in mid or later career, our younger colleagues will have to learn how to navigate through these rapidly shifting academic waters.

So far my comments have had to do primarily with what one might call the technological support environment of humanistic scholarship. Let me turn now to two subjects that get closer to the heart of things: first, to several issues of information access and second, to matters of research design and methodology. As younger humanists enter the academy they need above all to think carefully about the ways in which electronic information systems shape the very substance of the scholarly enterprise.

First, issues of bibliographic access. My understanding of these issues has been vastly expanded by the two years I recently spent in academic librarianship as University Librarian at the University of Minnesota. From the librarian's vantage point, it is clear that new technologies are profoundly affecting the ways we gain access to and establish conceptual control over the bibliographic information on which we so vitally depend. At my own university, the installation of a computerized library system containing an electronic database of all our catalogued materials, amounting to well over four and a half million volumes described by more than two million discrete records, has not only transformed how librarians operate—from cataloguing to reference work, from book purchasing to circulation control—but has altered the ways in which scholars identify and obtain the materials they need. I can now sit in front of my personal computer or stand before a public terminal in any of the library buildings and search the entire book collection instantly and by any combination of author, title, or subject keywords that I devise. In the near future I will also be able to search the contents of a vast array of journal literature as electronic indexes such as ERIC and MEDLINE are loaded on the library's computer. Before long, through the marvels of electronic networking, I will be able to call up a growing list of off-site bibliographic databases as well as the electronic records of over thirty research libraries in the Research Libraries Group consortium. A committee of RLG on which I sit is hard at work identifying special bibliographic databases that can be loaded on the consortium's Stanford-based computer for access by librarians and scholars at participating universities across the United States.

The prospect of virtually instantaneous access to such vast bibliographic riches is truly awesome. Electronically based bibliographic access is helping to create unparalleled research opportunities, for it enables us to survey more fully and promptly than ever before the literature that guides research initiatives and provides the intellectual context for their development.

Access eased, however, can quickly produce information overload. As the tide of scholarly output swells and interdisciplinary work demands increasing attention to diverse fields of knowledge, the task of sorting through the scholarly literature and establishing conceptual control over it becomes ever more difficult. The implications for graduate students struggling to achieve initial mastery of the literature in their field are clear. They must have access to the full range of bibliographic materials that modern electronic systems can provide and learn how those materials can be downloaded as working bibliographies into their personal computers. And yet they must learn as well to avoid the information glut that can paralyse initiative, especially for the beginning scholar.

If technology is transforming the informational landscape, it also has important implications for the questions that humanists ask and for how humanistic scholars design and carry through their work. I began this paper with the observation that the research paradigms and methods of the humanities have been less dramatically affected by information technology than those of the natural or social sciences. At the same time, the machine has important implications for what we understand humanistic scholarship to be. Here again, graduate students need to develop some understanding of these issues as they begin their research careers.

The interplay between research design and computer capabilities in the storage, retrieval, and manipulation of data is intimate and far reaching, if not always understood. Wherever large scale computer applications, especially computer based information systems, have taken place, they have served as agents of change in ways both intended and unforeseen.[21] Whether in industry, libraries, or universities, large scale information technologies rearrange how things are done, redistribute knowledge and thus reconfigure authority, and redefine organizational values. As members of university communities, humanists are affected by and need to understand the institutional changes that computer applications produce: for example, the shifting and often troubled relationships between academic and administrative computing; the appearance of chief information officers, often not academics themselves, who wield vast influence over all aspects of university information policy; or the strengthened ties of faculty members to research colleagues elsewhere, often at the expense of institutional loyalty.

When placed at the centre of scholarly activity, the machine can also alter the research agenda. Computer based data systems, for example, enable scholars to examine large collections of texts in ways that were not possible when those materials were physically dispersed and not electronically scannable. One thinks, for example, of the kinds of textual

---

21. See, for example, the penetrating discussion of computers and organizational change in Shoshana Zuboff, *In the Age of the Smart Machine: The Future of Work and Power* (New York: Basic Books, 1988).

analysis opened up by the Thesaurus Linguae Graecae, an electronic, natural language library of all surviving Greek literature from 759 BC to 600 AD containing over sixty two million words! Or the Packard Humanities Institute's plans to encode classical Latin texts. Or the ARTFL project at the University of Chicago with its plans to create a database of over 1,500 French language texts ranging from literary and philosophical works to scientific and technical texts. Or the Medieval and Early Modern Data Bank at Rutgers University containing European currency and notarial records from the 14th to the 16th centuries. The list could easily be expanded.[22]

Together these databases and their accompanying search software offer unparalleled opportunities for full text analysis, constructing detailed concordances, tracing the historical development of terms used in social discourse, or examining the evolution of linguistic structures and literary conventions over time. The Old Spanish Language Project, sponsored jointly by the University of Wisconsin and the University of California at Berkeley, extends research possibilities even further by bringing together in one integrated, hypertext environment a citation-based dictionary of the Spanish language prior to 1500 (an entirely new scholarly resource); a Bibliography of Old Spanish Texts listing the primary source materials from which the dictionary was derived; full text copies of the original manuscripts and incunabula listed in the bibliography; a Biographical Directory of authors, scribes, printers, and others associated with the original creation and distribution of those texts; and a descriptive listing of geographical place names contained in the texts or associated with their creation and use. The possibilities for scholarly analysis opened by these linked and cross referenced databases challenge the imagination.

Each of us could cite additional projects that we know about or in which we have an interest. The best of them will suggest entirely new questions to ask and generate new theories of linguistic or cultural change. If successful, each will channel scholarly resources and energy in newly productive ways.

And yet that channelling raises potentially troubling questions. The electronic accessibility of some materials rather than others will

---

22. These and other large scale information projects are described in Constance Gould, **Information Needs in the Humanities: An Assessment** (Stanford: Research Libraries Group, 1988).

influence the decisions scholars make about where to direct their energies for, as human nature and pressures of publication dictate, readily available information will be examined more frequently than information requiring collection and arrangement. In addition, the structure of data files, usually defined with specific research tasks in mind, may limit the questions that can effectively be asked of the database and further channel the inquiries that scholars pursue. Every database reflects a distinct universe of discourse based on assumptions concerning the discrete entities constituting the database and the anticipated relationships between them. No database is truly 'open' or 'neutral', but each is limited to inquiries of specific kinds. So it is with files of nineteenth century voting data as well as full text databanks of romantic poems or Roman inscriptions.[23]

Over time, the cumulative effect of research choices guided by data file structure and software capabilities may not only bias what we know, but create privileged ways of knowing. Something like that happened over the past several decades in an area that I know something about, US political history, where the quantitative analysis of American voting behaviour, carried forward initially by the imaginative linking of voting records, censuses and other social data, became in time a kind of privileged discourse that focused increasingly on methodological rather than historical issues and pushed other, non-quantitative modes of discourse into the background.

The cost-benefit ratio of large scale database development, moreover, needs to be carefully examined. The collection and encoding of full text databases and the development of software necessary to exploit them are expensive in both dollars and human time. This can create incentives to expand scholarly participation in a project in order to distribute and justify the costs, incentives that may exceed a project's broader significance.

The natural sciences are based on the premise that findings are not accepted as part of the scientific canon until they have been experimentally tested and replicated by other scholars. Thus numerous scientists often draw on the same or closely similar data to support their work. Humanistic scholarship, by contrast, is highly individualistic and

---

23. Sebastian Rahtz explores aspects of database theory in S. Rahtz (editor) **Information Technology in the Humanities: Tools, Techniques, and Applications** (New York: Halsted Press, 1987).

non-experimental. It tends not to concentrate scholarly attention on given databases or along similar lines of investigation, but to disperse inquiry across a variety of data sets, theoretical systems, and intellectual queries. While complex databases can often service numerous research agendas, the number of scholars eager to use any particular database may prove limited, especially over time as theoretical fashions and research agendas change.

Several other considerations raise questions about the long-term viability of large scale databases—for example, the necessary commitment to their continuous updating and expansion, a commitment that funding agencies, wary of financial 'black holes', are reluctant to make; and the inevitable moment when the project's scholarly founders shift their attention elsewhere.

In a paper in this volume (see above, p.52), Professor Connor reports regretfully that in spite of the remarkable riches of the Thesaurus Linguae Graecae and the fact that 'no other humanistic field (except perhaps linguistics) has comparable access to such comprehensive and sophisticated computerization' as does Classical Studies, most publications in the field's major journals fail to cite the database extensively. Nor has the new technology, he finds, opened up major new questions about the ancient world or provided fresh strategies for exploring familiar questions.

The difficulties posed for humanistic scholarship by these large ticket items scarcely equal the dilemmas posed by 'big science' projects such as the Hubbell Space Telescope or the Superconducting Supercollider. Would that humanists had to be concerned about costs so gargantuan! And yet within the modest world of humanities funding, questions need to be asked about the scholarly payoffs from different investments of scarce funding resources.

What does all of this have to say about the training of the modern scholar? In fact, a great deal. As young scholars become active in the shifting fields and subfields that constitute the humanities, they need to become familiar with computer based projects relevant to their own areas of inquiry so they can make informed decisions about utilizing them. More than that, emerging scholars have a special stake in the future management of information and thus will need to share in the important decisions about which projects go forward, which software developments have priority, and how the problems of scholarly access and cost management are to be addressed. As we all know, the list of worthy projects is essentially infinite while the resources available to support them are distressingly finite. Librarians and other information specialists, information vendors, and granting agency officials have justifiable claim to share in the decisions that are made. Those decisions, however, must be driven above all by the scholar's definition of what the research agenda should be. Developing the capacity to help define that agenda takes time; it is crucial that attention to these issues begins early in a young scholar's career.

If our future colleagues need help in learning how to utilize the technological environment that supports their work, how can that help best be provided? Answers to the question will vary, depending on the student's academic field and research agenda, the interests and competencies of graduate faculties, and levels of institutional support. Several issues, however, need to be addressed by whatever training strategy is devised.[24] One is the extent to which computer knowledge and competencies are to be nurtured by the student's general coursework and research as opposed to specially designed computer courses. Both surely are needed and the mix will vary in keeping with levels of faculty and student commitment to computer-assisted work.

More in dispute is what constitutes an appropriate introduction to humanistic research in the humanities—whether practical, hands-on familiarity with existing computer applications, training in the algorithmic logic that underlies programming and database theory, or the systematic design of research problems from question formulation and database design through data processing and analysis.[25]

The immediate gratification gained from running packaged programs against prepared databases may help overcome machine anxiety in some students and capture the game playing fancies of others, but it sends the false message that computer based inquiry has to do primarily with skills and software manipulations rather than with the ways in which question formulation, theory, data, and technique combine to produce knowledge.[26] More than the technical skills that computer applications make possible, young scholars need to think systematically about how the

---

24. Volume twenty one of Computers and the Humanities (1987) contains a valuable series of essays on computer courses for the humanities.

25. Robert Oakman explores this debate in 'Perspectives on teaching computing in the humanities'. Computers and the Humanities, 21 (1987) 227-233.

26. Nancy Ide makes this distinction forcefully in 'Computers and the humanities courses: philosophical bases and approach'. Computers and the Humanities, 21 (1987) 209-215.

machine, in all its dimensions, shapes as well as facilitates the work they do.

I have left until last the problem of funding support for new information technologies, both because of its complexity and its seemingly intractable nature. In the broadest sense, strategies for funding graduate student access to computer based information technologies differ little from those required for faculty support. Much depends on funding decisions at the university level—for example, support for library mechanization, telecommunications, and academic computer services. Here the interests of humanists, social scientists, and other academicians converge, and humanists should vigorously pursue these inter-university alliances of mutual convenience. Humanists should also promote university participation in information consortia such as the Research Libraries Group, for in this way institutional investments can be leveraged into larger scholarly advantage via networked information systems and the sharing of materials through interlibrary loan. No one has a higher stake in the success of such enterprises than humanists, given their heavy dependence on books and journals and the constantly rising costs of those materials.

What of graduate student access to personal computers? Though many universities now provide personal computers for faculty, computer availability for graduate students poses a more difficult problem, for graduate students are both more numerous and more transient in their ties to the university. In my own department, the problem has been at least partly solved by the creation of a computer lab, available to faculty and graduate students alike, staffed by several accomplished consultants, and funded out of a combination of university, departmental, and grant based resources. There students have access to wordprocessing, laser printing, and a variety of computational capabilities, including connection, on the few occasions when it is still necessary, to the university's mainframe system. Mainframe access costs related to regular courses of instruction are covered by the university's Academic Computer Service. In support of graduate research, the university provides $1,000 of computer time as a 'match' to each researcher's $50 investment. For computer research connected with Masters theses or doctoral dissertations, the History Department covers the $50 charge.

Finally, students and faculty in the Department of History have benefited from a several hundred thousand dollar National Science Foundation grant supporting cooperative research on the federal census of 1880. Though only a limited number of students are directly involved in the project, the equipment, software, and enhanced computer skills generated by the grant will benefit the department as a whole. Scientists learned long ago how to leverage broad advantage from cooperative research ventures. Humanists can take a lesson from their success.

Information technologies and the training of the modern scholar—the agenda continues to evolve. I have touched on but a part of it in this essay. We need to share with each other and with our students what we have done and learned, to our mutual advantage and the academy's future health.

The Dissemination of Scholarly Knowledge

Angela Blackburn

Oxford University Press

The ability to produce multiple copies of a work was concentrated in the hand of printers, by and large, from Caxton until the middle of the twentieth century. There have always existed other means of disseminating knowledge—the public lecture, for example, was the mainstay of medieval university teaching, and has remained popular until the present day. Radio and television have increased the power and range of verbal communication. Written text can be produced in standard readable form and copies made for distribution by various means, from typewriters with carbon paper to, more recently, the photocopying machine. These have all made it progressively easier to produce multiple copies relatively cheaply, without recourse to printers. But the challenge to the supremacy of conventional printing presented by 'new technology' in the form of the computer is perceived to be something of a different order.

Printing until the 1960s or 1970s was essentially an industrial process. The use of metal type in typesetting required a factory environment—a foundry was part of every printing house. There were physical constraints against typesetting at one site and printing at another, and the printing process itself involved vast, heavy machines. Since the mid-sixties printing technology has been progressively 'de-industrialized', and computer technology has played a key role in the later stages of this process. The advent of photolitho printing heralded the split between printing and typesetting (the printed image could be produced indirectly—'off-set'), but a key breakthrough was the invention of the simple IBM typesetter—essentially a glorified typewriter—which could produce acceptable camera-ready copy outside the factory environment at consequently low cost. Typesetting machines have developed and improved hugely in the last twenty years, through advanced applications of computer technology in both the storage and retrieval of information and the creation of sophisticated photo-images. The computer has been seen as the ally of the conventional printing process. But at the same time it has signalled the end of the monopoly of the publisher. It is now, in principle at least, possible for an author to produce his own camera-ready copy without the intervention of a publisher. Moreover, using purely electronic means he can distribute his text without the intermediary of print, by making it available 'online' or simply by mailing copies of his diskettes to his friends and acquaintances. The questions which now face us are: will conventional publishing disappear, and printed books vanish from the library shelves of the twenty-first century? And if so, should we be concerned about it—will this represent an improvement and an advance on the present state of affairs, or will we be losing something valuable?

The power of the printed word

It is not a particularly novel suggestion that the dominance of print has engendered certain quite rigid expectations of the nature and form of scholarly knowledge. Wisdom, we believe, comes in the shape of books. Primitive peoples may have disseminated their wisdom in the form of paintings or carvings on stone, in arrangements of rocks or giant mega-liths, or in the telling of tales, but only in very recent years have literate peoples believed in the serious cultural and informational content of these media and we are still a long way from understanding that content. For us, books dominate our conception of what is wise and true and worth preserving. And books have a certain shape and size. The range of formats which are or have ever been in common use is extremely limited. A book has to be portable, which lays some limits on its size and weight and hence the number of pages it may contain; the page size must be such that the whole page can be read from one position, without moving the body or head excessively; and so forth. The question 'How long is a book?' may seem as meaningless as the question 'How long is a piece of string?', but we all have a sense of the limiting cases which give either question a point. This sense informs our judgements of what counts as scholarly knowledge, 'a substantial intellectual contribution'; univer-sities require graduate students in the humanities to produce a disserta-tion which is book-length as a qualifying test of their ability to sustain a full programme of research. At a more mundane level we expect word-processing programs to come equipped with the sort of apparatus which has been developed to aid our use of books: footnoting programs, conventions to replicate italic or bold typesetting fonts, page numbers. Partly at least we need these conventions because at the end of the day we expect to print our text—print being still the dominant medium. But we are beginning to recognize that, with the advent of computer technology, our knowledge and the way it is disseminated may be organized and transmitted in a radically different way.

I will look at three different embodiments of 'scholarly knowledge', all in principle available in both electronic and paper media, and try to characterize the strengths and weaknesses of each mode of 'dissemination' and the implications for both publishers and scholars. These are: monographs; scholarly editions of texts; and databases. I will not discuss the myriad other types of book or types of publication—volumes of poetry, atlases, 'pop-up' books, wordprocessing programs, and so forth. This is partly because of constraints of space, but partly also because I believe that certain basic issues are raised with respect to these types of publication which may inform our subsequent attitudes towards a world in which 'electronic publication' will form an active part.

Monographs

In some ways, the monograph defines what we mean by 'book length'— long enough to present and sustain an original argument of some depth and complexity, to deal effectively with evidence and counter-evidence. To my mind, it is not purely coincidental that a monograph turns out to be something of about the same length as a novel; sometimes running into three volumes ('major') and sometimes being only 120 pages long ('short'), but as often as not falling between 200 and 500 pages in length. Would it be possible to publish a monograph in purely electronic form? One characteristic of the (good) monograph is that it has a beginning, a middle, and an end, like a novel; and one is generally expected to read it by starting at page 1 and reading through to the end. If it were regarded as something with purely 'informational content', then nothing whatever would be lost by having it in electronic form; searching the text for the desired bits of information would simply become a whole lot easier. But in the real case, the important dimension of heuristic and rhetoric will have been sacrificed—the power to engage the imagination, the persuasive power of a sustained and well-supported argument—and also the ability to refer forwards and backwards, in the context of an accepted order to the reading of the text. These are matters independent of the question of the physical difficulty of reading a text of any length on a computer screen, or alternatively printing out in cumbersome fashion from an electronic text-base, producing a version which is more readable than a screen but difficult to store (compared to a bound book). For many reasons, then, we would probably *prefer* our monographs to continue to appear in conventional book format.

We are faced, however, with shrinking library budgets and an explosion in the number of monographs being published. It is now no longer possible for a publisher to keep a monograph in print 'for ever'; three to five years is regarded as a decent life-span, and print-runs of 600 or 750 copies are not uncommon where ten years ago one might have expected to print 1,500 or 2,000 copies. So most good libraries may never acquire copies of most published monographs. In these circumstances, electronic storage and retrieval of this type of material, as a cheaper and more efficient means of dissemination, may seem to be an option worthy of serious investigation. Are there any dangers? Well, in the first place this was material we are presuming was planned as a book; disseminating it electronically makes it *standardly* available in a different way. There is no reason, for example, why a reader should standardly start at 'page 1' as the notion of a fixed page sequence itself may rapidly become redundant. The organization and probably the style of the material will become subject to a different set of rules, and this will inevitably affect the content. Secondly, the onus of protecting the author's copyright, and indeed preserving the purity of his text, will fall entirely on libraries or whoever is distributing it electronically. And being available electronically makes copying easy. Plagiarism occurs now; will it become a policing nightmare in the putative electronic library? This raises a further question, as to whether a scholar, who has devoted all his life to teaching and research, in other words to the dissemination of scholarly knowledge, might or should object to his ideas being disseminated broadly and without controls. Is he being in some way inconsistent to teach his ideas to his students and expect them to take them on board and to make them their own, and yet to object when others take over his thoughts by a different means? I will explore this later.

Scholarly editions

Here new technology poses a different set of problems. Let us take a text. It was published in the seventeenth century, 'underground', because it was political dynamite. It was pirated freely. Many of the pirated versions—all hand typeset, and all slightly different from the original—

carry the same printing date as the first impression, but some may incorporate significant changes authorized by the author. Familiar meat for the textual scholar. It may take that scholar twenty years of his professional life to establish an 'authoritative' text, and the effort and sacrifice may not be negligible. When published this edition will, under the accepted rules, be copyright. Now that it is possible to scan a text electronically we increasingly find scholars in Britain and America scanning copyright texts with little or no idea of the issues involved. The copyright question may not be clear because they are engaged in 'pure research' and are making no direct financial gain from their activities and believe themselves to be covered by the 'fair dealing' provisions of various copyright laws, which protect legitimate uses such as simply reading and recognizing the significant differences between one text and another and making use of that in subsequent research or publications. And in any event, the copyright text may differ in only small respects from any particular non-copyright version. But what is important about the copyright text is that it carries *authority*; others can take it, more or less on trust, that this is an accurate, complete, 'best' text. This is because the original scholar has done his work, has checked the details, and found them to be accurate.

Recently I came across a statement from a publisher of texts in electronic form, that he believed it to be legal to scan public domain works, then proofread them against copyrighted editions as long as discrepancies with original editions were noted. It is strange that such a procedure did not strike that publisher as an infringement of copyright, for, apart from the technology employed, such a case does not seem materially different from the case of an editor using *conventional* means to reproduce a text—re-keying the 1690 edition manually, for example, but correcting it where necessary against the 1990 (copyright) edition and simply footnoting to indicate discrepancies. A cumbersome process, no doubt, to re-key the whole text instead of simply scanning it, but the underlying principles are no different. And we also return to the paradox: why should the scholar, who laboured to produce the *best* text and wanted not to keep his knowledge to himself, but to have it disseminated widely and to be recognized as the best, object to other people by whatever means reproducing that text and using it or sharing it amongst themselves?

Databases

Here computers seem to come into their own. For computers can handle huge bodies of data with amazing ease; they can create bodies of data where none existed before. Every text is, on top of what it is as a text, also a repository of data—about the language in which it is composed, about its subject-matter, and so on. Not only can we, with the aid of computers, exploit these repositories of data with ease, we can also update and alter the data, compare it with other data, store it, send it across continents. A dictionary can be encompassed in a simple hand-held device that may be at the same time more portable and more versatile than its paper counterpart. Corpora of millions of words are being assembled which can be explored, analyzed, and reconstructed to make and to validate the dictionaries and grammar books of the future. Information of essential use to professional groups such as lawyers can be made available 'online' so that they can have access to it in absolutely up-to-date form, in a moment, anywhere they happen to be. As a research tool and as a means of disseminating knowledge, in this context the computer seems to outpoint conventional paper publishing. It is both faster—so the knowledge can be more up-to-date—and, in many and perhaps most contexts, more convenient to use.

I have mentioned dangers which might attend the other two means of disseminating knowledge under discussion, and both concern the ease with which an electronic text can be copied. That physical ease seems to make a difference to our attitude to electronic publication even though the underlying principles, concerning the right to copy, are the same as for conventional text. With databases this may also be a problem perhaps even more serious because the database may be perceived as having enormous commercial value, but there is an additional difficulty. The ease with which an electronic database can be updated may not be an advantage in every context. For it can be altered for the worse—mistakes can be introduced maliciously or accidentally—with equal ease; and of a number of alternative versions of the database, it may not be easy to tell which is the 'canonical' version, on which we should rely. And in addition, simply *accessing* the database may be regarded as an infringement of rights—in a way in which *accessing* a literary text is not.

Copyright

I have mentioned copyright and will now say a little more on this subject. Copyright law exists to protect an author's 'intellectual property'. I have suggested that it might seem paradoxical that a scholar, who has worked all his life, perhaps, to unearth some fund of knowledge, and who genuinely and disinterestedly wants other people to share his discoveries, should feel strongly about his property rights in that piece of knowledge. Tutors do not open their tutorials with a warning against breach of copyright and students who demonstrate that they have acquired the knowledge their teachers wanted to impart are rewarded with high marks and good degrees. Nevertheless there is a general understanding of what counts as 'fair dealing' in the context of using and disseminating knowledge. We need to examine this more closely and to ask whether our conventions have any real purpose in a community of scholars and whether new technology makes a difference to our perception of these issues, which makes it necessary to sharpen our intuitions or make our definitions more precise.

The most obvious purpose of copyright legislation may seem to be to protect the financial aspect of publication. The author's text is a piece of *property*; it can be bought and sold in published form. This may make some money for the author; if anyone uses the text without paying for it he is denying some revenue to the author. It may also make some money for the publisher, so one can understand why publishers are fierce about protecting their authors' copyrights. For high-level scholarly works the direct financial benefit to the author and the publisher may be negligible or negative, but both may benefit financially in an indirect way—perhaps the author may earn advancement in his career, and perhaps the publisher may enhance his status through the publication so that more lucrative projects are attracted into his fold. But books are expensive; and it is just those high-level scholarly works which are the most expensive. New technology, applied to conventional book production, was supposed to make things cheaper, but instead the prices of books have gone up and up. The suggestion has been raised, therefore, whether new technology ought not to *replace* conventional book production. Text or data could be transmitted from computer to computer for free (virtually). This might undermine our conventions about copyright; and the question has been raised as to whether this might not be a good thing, because knowledge ought to be free, that wide dissemination is one of the aims of scholarship and copyright may simply be an artefact of a materialistic world.

There are certain important factors which this kind of argument may overlook. One is that conventional publication makes knowledge *attributable*. This means that the source of the knowledge can be recognized and acknowledged; and also that the source of errors can be recognized and acknowledged. Both are important. It could be argued that the real value of our conventions about copyright is in just this; and the financial implications are secondary. For any piece of knowledge we want to know not just what it is but where it came from. The student who hits upon the right answer by sheer guesswork is not held to be entitled to claim that as knowledge. And we need to be able to investigate and verify the claims of serious researchers, to check that the accepted body of knowledge is securely based. The vision of a world in which a stream of knowledge, ever-changing, ever-updated, is freely available, is not one which a serious scholar would necessarily welcome; certainly not one who is detached from independent means of validation of the knowledge presented.

In addition, conventional publication means that the body of knowledge is available, in principle, to everybody who needs it, and not just to an 'in-group' who are friends of the author, or who belong to some similar closed network. And it is available in the same form; it is recognizably the same body of knowledge. So the person in a distant country or an underprivileged society, is not especially disadvantaged when it comes to gaining access to that knowledge, as he might be if it existed, for free maybe, but unpublished in a true sense.

In the course of enlarging the community of knowledge in this way, publishers can also reaffirm and monitor *standards* of knowledge. Much of a scholarly publisher's work will be in subjecting book proposals to proper scrutiny, to ensure that what is published meets the appropriate and accepted standards. So the reader in a remote country can rely on the quality of the product as securely as the reader close to the fountainhead of knowledge.

This is not intended as an argument against 'electronic publication', but simply to raise the question, how far can these aspects of conventional publication be preserved in the new medium?

Conclusion

It might be thought that computers provide the means to disseminate knowledge virtually for free. We might look forward to a glorious future when the conventional monograph or reference work has disappeared from the scene, library budgets have been liberated (maybe there will be no libraries), and everybody has access to whatever knowledge is available via some simple keyboarding operations. I have argued that this is a naive vision. The control conventional publishers exert at present, or are instrumental in exerting (because it is always the scholars themselves who do the refereeing of book proposals and typescripts), over standards of quality and consistency of product are needed more than ever in a world where the quantity of information has expanded exponentially and the readers have less and less of the time and perhaps even skill to evaluate by themselves the quality of what is provided.

Computer technology has hit the world with comparative suddenness, and we are still working out the ground rules for operating with it. What I argue is that, on examination, there is no very strong reason why the ground rules should be radically different from the rules that have operated hitherto. The fact that new technology makes it suddenly enormously more easy to copy someone else's works does not essentially change matters. For years publishers have not had a monopoly of the means of making multiple copies of texts. And we do understand that the paradox I have mentioned, of the scholar who *wants* the results of his research to be disseminated, and does not expect any direct financial gain, nevertheless objecting to others obtaining that material by unconventional means, is only an apparent paradox. There is a jealousy of knowledge and a pride in labour which must be appeased. The scholar will give up his knowledge freely to those of *good faith*, but reluctantly to scavengers. This feeling is based on a sense of community of interest. Only if disseminators of electronic texts show that they are sensitive to this will they continue to be able to make use of the work of scholars. And this may involve a closer adherence to the rules and conventions of the traditional publishing world than might appear at first sight.

Conclusions

Computers and the Humanities: a Personal Synthesis of Conference Issues

D.F. McKenzie

Oxford University

Our concern about the impact of new technology on human activity as recorded in the humanities is not unprecedented. Nor are the problems we find in explaining it. The technology of speech, for example, as Thomas Hobbes pointed out, was by far the most important for the development of human society. I am not sure how many centuries ago one might place its arrival, nor indeed how quite to define its distinction from the grunts, squeals, cries of distress, and laughter with which we still order some of our (I think most important, certainly our most intimate) social relationships. Yet for all our experience of speech, and our extraordinary range of competences in it, we cannot yet fully explain its functions. Despite even the most impressive achievements of computational linguistics, I am sure that Professor Zampolli would be one of the first to admit that our knowledge of the exact nature of linguistic transactions is still very limited.

But nor are we in any better case with the technologies of literacy. The manner in which the advent of writing changed the nature of social relationships (as distinct from the ways in which we might now from written record 'know' past societies) is also far from clear. As Professor Connor said, the advent of that technology is much discussed, but exactly how once wholly oral communities accommodated it and then exploited it, and precisely how it was thought to record and then to form experience, remains—even after some two to three thousand years—something of a mystery. Not being a classicist I do not have the classicist's advantage in the generation of hypotheses, namely the absence of extensive and compelling evidence. By contrast, as a native of a country whose indigenous Maori population, though literate, prefers to communicate orally even in most formal situations, I am all too aware of the problems of defining cultural difference in terms of those competitive means of record and address. Their political, and economic, implications are forced upon one daily, and yet their role in social relations is so complex as to frustrate all but the most self-evident explanations. It is certainly not to be defined in terms of our own easy, not to say slippery, shifts between speech and written text.

The technology of the codex—far more sophisticated I believe than Professor Landow allows in his concern to stress the advantages of hypertext—and its further sophistication by the technologies of print, are also imperfectly understood. If the historical conditions of their introduction and their myriad uses continue to fascinate, it is at least in part because we still cannot explain them. And yet printing from movable types has been with us in Europe since the mid-15th century. The paradox is similar to that of speech: we are superbly adept at using it, but mere amateurs at accounting for its nature in its effects. How, in short, *do* we read? But we do.

One could go on to the technologies of image creation and their associated industries, of the recording and transmission of sound, of the visual representation of motion—all of them technological innovations fundamental to the simulation of human experience. The olfactory and the tactile dimensions of experience are still difficult to capture in a machine, though smell I suspect might well prove in time to be a highly significant element in our (currently all too sanitized) forms of recovering the past. And tactile experience is an enormously valuable way of receiving and imparting information. If it were not, there would be even more divorces. But the point is not trivial: in the arts, the aesthetic object demands to be seen and felt.

My points then are quite simple. First, I find little that is so distinctive to computing technology that one cannot find a precedent for it in earlier technologies. Second, our knowledge of the past suggests that explanations of the kind this conference has been seeking have always proved partial, theoretically unsatisfying, and therefore unpredictable. And yet, third, those technologies—of speech, literacy, print, sound, and image transmission—have, pre-eminently, served the creation, transmission and reception of that class of texts we associate with *Humanitas*. Their historically very recent appropriation by science, along with computing technology, should not blind us to the long affinity of *Humanitas* with *Techne* as the very condition of their permanence, and therefore of their capacity to go on speaking to successive generations. In doing that, they constitute our collective memory.

That memory—it is essential to stress—is of a quite different order from the one now offered by computers, whose function is to record in order to analyze. In literature and the arts its function is to record in order to preserve, recover and renew. It thereby enables us to remake the past in the ever-changing complex of human experience; and in that generative capacity for renewal every time we consult 'the thing itself' we discover its value in informing the present. (Take any book from the shelf, it will give you back your self.) Such a memory, in the form of pre-existent texts, sounds and images, however we shape them to our own needs, is, in Marvell's words, an

> ocean where each kind,
> Does straight its own resemblance find.

Science gained the initiative in using computers simply because they were then such primitive tools: they could add and subtract at speed, but had no memory adequate to the complexities of natural language and aesthetic compositions. It was only when computers developed a memory of sorts that the humanities could even begin to accept that they might be of some use. But, again, let us not confuse the kinds of memory each has. Unlike computer-memory, which must homogenize the physical data, and establish links within it, the humanist memory bank is constituted by discrete physical objects which inhabit a quite different space and directly encode all the signs of their distinctive constructions. They are palpable, tangible, and in almost all cases they are proportioned to a human scale. They know what it is not to be over-ambitious in the human resources of time, space or professional training they command. Their power as a memory lies in a paradox: their relative stability (it is much the *same* artefact we pick up, look at, put down, return to the shelf; it is made from *those* words, colours, shapes, sounds, in *that* paper, paint, stone, or mix of instruments), and yet their expansive capacity to generate an infinite variety of responses. In Professor Zampolli's terms, they are a large repository of re-usable linguistic (and/or visual and tactile) information representing knowledge in a poly-theoretical way. And unlike computers and their products they already have a dynamic presence and historical depth within the culture.

Some of the artefacts that constitute the humanities memory bank are of course more active than others, but their physical existence, as distinct products of conditions we may again come to find interesting, because responsive to current needs, will always enable—as Foucault put it—the restoration of subjugated knowledges or, in the title of an early 17th century book, the restitution of decayed intelligence. Foucault's phrase sums up, in effect, the Re-naissance itself and the birth of the very concept of *Humanitas*. That concept is quite alien to the ways in which computers are used to service the evanescent moment. The proliferation of incomplete, unenterable, and technologically irrecoverable databases, as project after project fails in its promised largesse, testifies to the problems this particular technology has in making history of and in itself. What is past in that brave new world is generally beyond recall.

By contrast then with the brief lives of computer-memory, whose function is essentially analytic, the analyses of human behaviour are already there in the humanities, formulated in the rhetorical structures of the texts (by which I mean all forms of recorded information) as distinct artefacts. It is the resource from which we confirm the continuities of human experience and extend it in ways most congenial to ourselves.

And there are no rules to privilege one construction over another. Institutions can create rules, which are forms of prediction, and then demand that students play by them if they want a good degree and the achievement of status in the same or a similar institution. But that is irrelevant to the nature of humanist texts as literary artefacts or aesthetic objects in the real world of writers, artists, musicians and—in every sense—readers. In that relation, an author asks of a reader, listener, or viewer only the minimum courtesy of attending to the work itself—and as a layman, as (in Johnson's phrase) a common reader. Again, in that relation, the computer has nothing to offer. In the sciences it may be used to predict and to verify: the very nature of literature and the arts and our responses to them preclude both functions.

Some of course do see lay experience and natural language transactions as regressive from the standards aspired to by professionals in their computer applications. For myself I happily acknowledge the lay person's natural capacity to respond directly to sophisticated literary or visual or aural structures. Even at the most banal, commercial level, it is the necessary condition of the continued production of literary texts or aesthetic forms. But my reasons for that belief are also grounded in personal experience. In the study of literature, I suppose I must pretend to something like professional knowledge. In music, I can freely confess that I am a fool—though I hope a holy one. I am not professionally informed about music, but even at the level of my relatively unsophisticated enjoyment of it, I could not live without it. The isle in *The Tempest* might well be 'full of noises,/Sounds, and sweet airs, that give delight and hurt not'; but on my desert island I would be lost without discs. And Bach, I would like to think, would not have had it otherwise: his music addressed his congregations and their musically lay successors as Shakespeare's plays have addressed his myriad theatrically lay audiences for the last four hundred years.

If there is a crisis in the humanities it is not in funding (though now I think of it, over-funding may indeed be a problem), it is in the antagonisms between artists and academies, the sense artists have that their works are appropriated and their distinctive roles diminished. ('Crisis' and 'critics', it is worth observing, have the same root.) What 'the Humanities' (a term that implies institutionalization and all its professional concomitants as *Humanitas* does not), what 'the Humanities' *do* to texts—most notably now perhaps with computers—is all too often seen by the very people with whom they originated as a betrayal, a gross distortion of the natural relation between author, text and reader-viewer-auditor. In so far as computer applications to the process of reading compound such betrayals, they are a destructive force. Put more politely, one might say they redefine the text and its uses in order to make them computable.

And that reflection takes us in one sense to the heart of the (false, because really institutional and therefore managerial) problem: how we define the humanities. From the perspective of the definition I have been implying, essentially a literary one, the conversions offered by computers can all too easily deform the artefact and thereby distort the terms of the relationship between the work itself and the conditions proper to its reception—unless, of course, like much new music, it is computer-generated. From the perspective of the social sciences, however, computers offer possibilities for recording and analyzing information on a scale quite unprecedented; fields of social and economic inquiry in particular can now, and realistically so, be far more extensive; and that scale and the attendant technologies of networking permit collaborative projects. While the accumulation of information and the problems of interpreting it create their own risks of distortion, and the relative impersonality of collaborative work can create an illusion of objectivity enlarging the pitfalls of induction, any conjectures are more open to refutation by the same methods.

Given those two rather different ends of the spectrum, it is possible to see their collapse into 'the Humanities' (since, as we like to claim, '*humani nihil alienum*': more properly, Terence's '*homo sum: humani nil a me alienum puto*') as a risky stratagem. Such apparent solidarity can have its corporate advantages when it comes to bidding against the sciences for scarce resources. Its danger lies in the suppression of distinctions when those very distinctions are what define literature as not-history or not-linguistics or not-philosophy, let alone not-statistics. If we are to make a proper judgement at this conference about how best to use computers in our common interest, it seems to me essential that we begin by accepting and respecting the quite different nature of each of our disciplines within 'the Humanities'.

So far at this conference I have had the impression that the author-artist exists only as an economic obstacle in the form of copyright. That kind of reductivism, like the collapse into 'the Humanities', is of course consonant with other fashionable consequences of what Professor Miller has called the 'triumph of theory' (see above p.13)—a triumph some might prefer rather to describe as a Pyrrhic victory. Theory, if I may so collectively term it, has joined forces with institutional and economic imperatives in ways which I see expressed in three concerns of the conference. One is that, like managerial imperatives, it directs attention to the relationship between humane letters, history, and the social sciences. Another is therefore the presumed virtues of collaboration, dictated by the range of quite different professionalisms, as distinct from solitary creation. A third is the prominence given to one of the forms of expressing that convergence of interests in the analytical/re-constructive powers of something like hypertext as an interpretative tool, a way of reading, a form of commentary, a model (dare I suggest?) for scholarship.

What links those concerns is the assumption that all texts are less the product of a single author than they are social products. If that seems self-evident, it still needs to be made explicit: first, because the relation of a singular author to a multiple community is a paradox we cannot will away in a rush of technology and self-indulgent theorizing; second, because it reveals the assumed basis of many computer-designed forms of inquiry and judgement. As with memory, analysis, and predictability, we can locate here another kind of relationship to computing where the application of computer-based assumptions may be inimical to the very nature of humane letters.

Thus: if texts always were and always are social products, then their authorship always was and is collaborative. For artefacts from the past which we study now, we must therefore recover the multiple conditions of their making. We must therefore recreate with as much sophistication as possible the full complexities of context. It follows that inquiry into the non-linguistic or aesthetic elements of the artefact might benefit from the manner in which historians and social scientists recover and study such evidence. In so far as that evidence is on a scale beyond our individual capacity to record and retrieve it, the need to explain presupposes the need to compute.

The further presumption that the complexities are such that they can only be addressed by collaborative enterprise therefore reinforces the disposition to use tools perhaps more proper to the products of those other disciplines. The objection to that distortion is not one of logic, but one of judgement.

So too is the objection to literary-critical arguments which demote the author and his or her originating and rhetorically directive role. It is no contradiction of arguments for the text as a social product. It is simply that the logical consequences of some theories lead us into an absurdity from which the natural commonsense logic of the layman happily preserves him. Again, to be driven here by theory involves either a failure of critical judgement to locate the true object of inquiry or—another way of putting it—a conversion of that object to purposes quite different from those it was ostensibly created for. Happily, librarians still think that a concept of authorship as single, not multiple, is the most efficient way of organizing access to the texts of the past, even if the attribution of works to a single author is really (again in Foucault's words) only a sort of commonsense principle of economy in controlling the proliferation of meanings. Living authors, artists, and copyright lawyers also help.

Nevertheless, the theory of multiple or fragmented authorship informs the creation of structures such as hypertext to express multiple relationships. We may choose, say, Tennyson, but only as the construction of all the other elements of the system. Hypertext as a form of exposition is of course computer-dependent. Does it thereby serve or betray the essential nature of the literary text or aesthetic object?

It is my contention that it betrays the objects I know as literary. Let me immediately concede that all recorded texts are of course multiply-authored in the sense that they're the product of parchment or paper makers, masons, cameramen, instrument makers, recording engineers, software designers, teachers of reading and writing, of the communal stock of precedent rhetorical forms, the succeeding collaborative contributions of all transmitting agents, and the constructions of performers-readers-viewers-auditors. They are the product of social acts involving the intervention of human agency acting on the material forms.

For that very reason (the fact that texts are indeed social products), the forms themselves encode the history of their production. It follows that to abstract a conceptual or verbal information content from them by representing them in another medium is to contradict the very assumption that the artefact is the product of a distinctive complex of materials, labour and mentality. In so far as the forms themselves are simulations (as Plato long ago objected) their re-presentation in a database—a copy of a copy—is an impoverishment, a theft of evidence, a denial of more exact and immediate visual and tactile ways of knowing, a destruction of their quiddity as collaborative products under the varying historical conditions of their successive realizations. In other words, there is an internal contradiction enforced by the very conditions of the medium used—computing—to simulate the very conditions to be examined. By contrast, libraries (shall we say, along with museums and art galleries), by giving us direct access to the artefacts themselves (encoded as they are with all the signs of their production), thereby minimize the distortions of further re-presentations. One concedes the necessity at times to use copies but resists the impulse (simply because computers make it possible) to build systems which involve, as it were, cumulative distortions.

But the point of entry to those comments was a theory of authorship as collaborative, as distinct from the traditional humanities model of an individual creator. Since I believe it is both single and multiple, let me simply suggest that the real terms of the distinction are temporal. Collaborative or group authorship, here and now, is in my experience fraught with difficulties. I am not the least bit defensive or apologetic about the writer-artist-humanist as isolate, but celebrate that happy state of withdrawal from family, colleagues (especially colleagues) into the conventional privacies of the library where the notion of a community of scholars is so pleasantly alive under conditions which recognize at the same time your right to work alone.

> Such was that happy garden state
> When man there walked without a mate.

But that is not to dispose of the notion of collaborative authorship: what I am resisting as necessarily desirable is the idea of concurrency. In the humanities, the most efficacious form of collaboration has always been sequential. It gives all the pleasures of controlling your own forms of work, and doing it at your own pace, while collaborating with all those writers, artists, and scholars who have preceded you. The model, again, is the library, in its historic depth. It is a proven way of enabling our participation in sequential collaboration. To displace that form of collaboration, so distinctive to the arts in their dialogue with the past as 'tradition', with one of concurrency is to insist on a radical change which has little to do with the objects at the heart of the humanities and much to do with antithetical economic and technological pressures.

The advantages of wordprocessing are beyond question: they are more than adequate to the scholarship of humane commentary on literary artefacts, and they can help in quite sophisticated ways in constructing critical editions. What is essential is that we retain a freedom of inquiry *beyond* the power of computers to serve. The danger lies in limiting our questions to those only computers can help us to answer.

Translated into practical decisions about the range of research in the humanities, that demands a fine judgement of ends and means, itself an essential element in research training. Of some 200 students beginning research projects in the English Faculty in Oxford over the last four years, very few so conceived of the tasks they thought it interesting or proper to do as humanists that they demanded sophisticated computer programs or collaborative databases. Yet their topics included inquiries into the textual problems of constructing and presenting subtitles in films for the hard-of-hearing (in relation to the image seen) and for non-English films (in relation to the language heard); Conrad's *Heart of Darkness* as it evolved for its readers in its first slow episodic appearance in the successive monthly contexts of non-canonical writers, mixed genres, and advertisements in a late-19th century periodical; Montgomery Clift, actor, as film text; the political implications of maps as texts; typographical experimentation in the post-structuralist American novel; the construction and promotion of the Sex Pistols' 'Anarchy in the UK' as a way of exploring distinctions between (indeed the very validity of the terms) 'high' and 'low' culture, an inquiry directly relevant to the question of the centrality to the humanities of the 'lay' man or woman as distinct from the professional.

For each of those students such topics were all the direct expression of, and the means of getting into focus, problems important to them as individuals. Imaginatively they are extraordinarily fertile, and perfectly adequate to the devising of computer-assisted analyses had they but thought these proper. What I have been impressed by is the judgement they show in their selection of means. All they ask for is access to the artefacts, the texts themselves. They resist the re-location of their reading spaces. They resist secondary simulations. They resist being over-whelmed by having secondary evidence in database form. If they want a group project, they hold a seminar, make a concert, put on a play, or join an audience. If they wish to extend their studies, they prefer to do so by extending and varying their aesthetic experience. That means working in several media, not comparatively (another compulsion of the computer-based mentality) but with a proper respect for the distinct nature of the ways in which printed and spoken language, images static and kinetic, music and dance, encode forms of experience whose value is realized only in their own terms. That is what seems to matter most to those students in the humanities, and I have no wish to persuade them otherwise.

For their resistance and the judgement that informs it are profound. By contrast, so much of what I hear about computing applications reminds me of the story of the staff officer who, when promised another man for his unit, replied: 'Send me one who is brilliant and energetic. If you can't do that, send me one who is brilliant and lazy. If you can't do that, send me one who is stupid and lazy. But for God's sake don't send me one who is stupid and energetic.'

Keith Devlin recently pointed out (*The Guardian*, 1 March 1990) that information technology is like the Cheshire Cat's grin: the world is increasingly organizing itself around things which do not actually exist. In a sense that has always been the case in the arts, where the truest poetry is the most feigning. But the human realizations of its fictions are a much more powerful form of virtual reality. In Sidney's words, they are 'another Nature', and can be known only through the very forms of their construction. In that, they are products utterly distinctive from those a database yields, 'things that are not'. My students want, in the terms the artists choose, the real thing; and that means the artefacts. I see little here to confirm Professor Miller's prediction that there will be radical changes in the ways in which we will read literature. Doubtless there will be some, though I suspect that the writers' response to such changes will be to force us back to traditional forms of narrative control.

When the great computer architect Von Neumann asked, many years ago, 'Can we survive technology?' (*Fortune*, June 1955), he made the point that computer technology is enormously generative: instead of performing the same task in half the time, it performs twice as much in the same time. Computer output therefore rapidly pre-empts space. It is important to gloss the word 'space', for it also stands now for the *dis*placement of non-computing projects in budgets, research proposals, equipment bids, as well as in hard discs and hard-copy printout. It may also displace thought. A wrong program (that is, a mistaken assumption in the program) will, with a mad logic, be more prodigal of error; and that prodigality will crowd out the often more severely disciplined, or simply more appropriate, evidence of other kinds of analysis. That risk is so great, it seems to me, that at least in some disciplines within the humanities, we are in urgent need of thinking through a definition of the 'national good' derived from a shared conviction of our distinctive needs.

Here I return to libraries. It has been my argument in this talk that in the humanities it is the product of the writer's, artist's or scholar's labour, the objects themselves, that are central. Collecting, classifying, preserving and offering access to them is our prime duty, and we fulfil that duty by enabling libraries to perform it as their prime task. Such a role is democratic in permitting every individual who wishes to realize a text from the past in his or her own way. It is collaborative both in so qualifying the past and in providing new work for the future to draw on and adapt. It is inter-textual in servicing all inquiries about the relations between any or all the objects a library holds. It is economic in multiplying the use and therefore the uses of each object. And in that last, mediating role, by dispersing the cost, it enables the common reader, the grant-starved student, the retired and dispossessed researcher, a guaranteed re-usable resource. Even its traditional commitment to published work has a continuing force, for publication in book form makes the invisible college visible.

But the final question is this: how can the applications and products of computer technology best serve those functions? Clearly any response must be two-fold. First, the computer is a superb tool for accessing data of a certain kind and, in the short term, retrieving it. It just happens that the kind of *managerial* data libraries must work with, and the long-proven principles for ordering it, is in the form of catalogues: descriptions of the artefacts themselves, their principal distinguishing features as physical objects, and their locations. That information has highest priority. The next stage is simply to maximize it—a task for which computers are the perfect tool—nationally and internationally, and (a point of crucial importance in the humanities) retrospectively, for *there* lies our memory. In terms of that argument, internal computerized services for readers in the form of specialized databases for the further satisfaction of those functions, and even forms of optical retrieval as a conservation strategy, are subordinate.

The second part of any response must be the library's responsibility to acquire and service non-library information in computerized form as characteristic 'textual objects' of our own time. And here we enter a shadow line; for it is here that, if libraries are to gather such texts, structure them, and give access to them, libraries must change.

To my mind, one of the most encouraging features of the conference has been a pervasive disenchantment with the products of computing applications. For therein lies the beginning of wisdom. Given such experience, many of those present have readily acknowledged that we must sharpen our judgement about the kind of inquiry it is proper to make in the humanities, improve the tools, improve the standards for the definition and storage of electronic texts, and avoid the need for software dependency—all of which seems to me eminently sensible. It recognizes a principal condition of the products of Humanitas that libraries have always served: the re-usability of artefacts and, in their hospitality to polytheoretic inquiry, their continuing usefulness to those beyond their creators. In that, we have a way of defining the further limits of the shadow line: the standards libraries should demand of computer-generated texts if they are to gather, structure and access them.

When, some 260 years ago, an earlier form of science and technology crept up on Alexander Pope, only to be abused by Dunces, he described its effect on the humanities in a text which is still eminently re-usable:

> Thus at her felt approach, and secret might,
> *Art* after *Art* goes out, and all is Night...
> *Philosophy*, that lean'd on Heav'n before,
> Shrinks to her second cause, and is no more.
> Thy hand, great Anarch! let's the Curtain fall
> And universal Darkness buries all.

The Anarch now is the dispenser of funding, unless—knowing the distinctive values of *Humanitas* as defined by its texts in all media—the current anarchy is rapidly succeeded by a form of government that restores to libraries their proper status and value as the embodiment of our communal memory. If, in our competitive pursuits of unrealizable goals, we frustrate that essential recognition, then a new Dark Age is upon us, and I for one would despair of an early renaissance.

Closing Address: the Role of the National Library

J.M. Smethurst

The British Library, Humanities & Social Sciences

I have been asked several times in this Conference what I hope to see emerge, and what I wanted to get out of it. It is not an easy question to answer, and in any event the answer may not be of any relevance to any of you. You may even rightly say the question is of no relevance either.

On the other hand, I think it is important to my work to let you know why I thought it right to act as Organizing Chairman of the Conference, and to tell you why the Conference is of importance from my specific viewpoint as Director General of what I believe to be the world's greatest Library for the Humanities and Social Sciences.

I think it is vitally important that I should direct my library entirely for the benefit of the scholars who need to use it. I can only do that properly if I can engage in a full dialogue with you in what you expect as the proper support from a research library in the furtherance of your work. But I have an obligation beyond your needs. I have, in my trust, the support from my library to the next generation of scholars, to the historian of the 21st century, and to the literary scholar of 100 years from now for the material we hold from the past and for the literature of the 1990s which will by then have been reassessed as part of the history of literature to the year 2100. I have responsibility to provide data, both from the evidence of the printed map and from the evidence of the electronic maps which are now replacing them, and for ensuring that the evidence is preserved in an accessible form. It is a responsibility which I cannot guarantee that others will undertake. Nor would I be fulfilling or meeting my responsibility if I allow my resources to be diverted to heavy expenditure to meeting a demand for current material of temporary value which will be superseded, or which will not be accessible because of changes of technology in the future. I believe that I have a responsibility, then, either to make provision in my library for the proper collection, preservation and access to the primary and secondary materials for humanities research, or to ensure that if I am not making that provision, the responsibility is held by some other body.

I am deeply concerned that the selectivity in acquisition which limited resources dictate should be sensitively practised, that it should be governed by an informed understanding of the priorities you set, tempered by my best professional assessment of your own foresight and wisdom in your understanding of the right mainstream priorities for resource support for the materials you need for your research. We cannot predict the future utility for material we acquire with any certainty—we should not presume to—but neither can we collect and make available everything. I have I believe in my keeping the most effective databank ever created and one which has proven utility—a very large research library of documents and books. If I am troubled about how we should select wisely, I am even more deeply troubled by what I fear to be the destructive qualities of our present condition, and the lack of direction, pressure and sustained and consistent political lobbying to improve it.

Professor Kenny in his opening address talked of the chain of research, and the interdependence of the links in that chain. He also identified the problems of technology in the humanities in terms of redundancy of effort, diversion of effort, diversion of funding, distortion of research, transfer of populations. To my mind the Conference has confirmed these to be the problems—and I believe it has shown that we are at a point of crisis and choice. With wisdom, foresight, and will, we can tackle the problems and avoid disaster to any part of the chain which failure to address the problems can bring. But to do this needs purposeful collaborative effort, and we, as librarians and researchers, cannot work within the isolation of our discipline or within the false comfort of the boundaries or our institutions or departments. Yet the lack of resources, the competitive pressure of the economic realities and political context in which we work may hinder that collaboration. I am worried that those utilitarian pressures which will direct funding will also distort research. I am concerned that those same pressures will also lead to the destruction of the concept of the great research library as an essential repository of the recorded knowledge of the age, and perhaps more importantly as the repository of the historical continuity of knowledge, of cultural achievement in its various formats. It is a repository or if you prefer, a database, which enables historical reassessment to be made, which can be entered at any point in time to examine the contemporary evidence and to reassess it from the viewpoint of today. It should also be the repository for material in new formats, for electronic data. But such material is not covered by the legislation for legal deposit, which predates the publication of material in these forms, and increasingly material of value in electronic format will not be archived and will be lost to future generations. (Unless, of course, there is a change in the legislation).

The computer has been a tool used by libraries for some twenty five to thirty years. We have made bad mistakes, many false starts, and wasted much money. But we have gone through the learning curve, and we are now beginning to deliver systems which offer the opportunity to scholars to have more effective knowledge of and less costly access to materials in all formats, irrespective of place. We have, I think, begun to appreciate fully the use of a computer as an enabling tool to achieve our goals of universal access and universal bibliographical control, and the benefits that the computer can also bring to the research process by enabling new types of research to be conducted. We are constructing bibliographical databanks which are used with increasing confidence and enthusiasm. We can develop international networks to give access locally to data in library collections held in machine readable form in any library. And those same catalogues can be analyzed in new ways by computer search and by reassembly of selected data.

The humanities scholar has the prospect before him of hitherto unrealizable access to the basic materials for his research. We must continue to build the bridges between networks in Europe and the United States. Yet we are in danger of failing the future scholar by failing to construct the properly resourced library for the future. We cannot undertake universal retrospective conversion, because we lack resources, but we have not collaborated fully with scholars in selecting what we should do; we fail to collaborate because we too are dominated by the pressure of response to an immediate utilitarian justification—we devote resources to expensive local provision when there is good national provision, we fail to contribute to a national resource because our institutions are becoming more competitive for their share of a limited overall resource. We lose the battle for acquisition of that which is of permanent value but inevitably of low use in favour of that which is of temporary value but thought to be of better immediate use. We measure by usage, not by value of use, and we are driven by the financial accountants, and to some extent by inappropriate performance measures into destructive policies.

I do not want libraries to become merely the providers of information—nor, I suspect, do you. But neither do I want libraries to be museums, preserving the past with no regard for service. I want them to be responsive energetic providers of the real needs of research, to give access and to share the responsibility for the provision with those who do the research. The research chain in the humanities must be strengthened, and my hope is that this conference is a first step in improving that strength. We can see the dangers, and we have had exciting insight into the opportunities. We must now go forward to exploit the technology, to recognize its potential as a powerful tool to enable research, and to achieve, where appropriate, new conditions for research. But in doing so, we must maintain a strong commitment to the long, distinguished and, in respect of the improvement of the human condition, totally pertinent tradition of preserving and maintaining the materials and artefacts which are the record on which so much research in the humanities depends.

I want to see what Dick de Gennaro stated so clearly, that the national library is the sum of the nation's libraries. And I want to see each as part of a wide area network, interconnected. We are making progress, but not fast enough, nor necessarily with a far-sighted understanding of the potential for the scholar of tomorrow.

Resolutions adopted at the Conference on Scholarship and Technology in the Humanities, held at Elvetham Hall, 9-12 May 1990

The conference agreed that it was essential that scholars have easy access to the widest possible range of scholarly materials in all types of format, and that the academic and library communities needed to work together to preserve and defend such access in a period of growing crisis. The conference identified several problem areas which needed urgent attention at national and international levels, and passed the following resolutions:

1. The retrospective conversion of manual catalogues of holdings of printed texts, manuscripts and artefacts should proceed as rapidly as possible in order to provide greater access and bibliographic control.

2. To this end there should be international cooperation and division of labour, especially in the construction of national union catalogues and national authority files.

3. Encouragement should be given to international electronic links and online access to national bibliographic databases.

4. In view of the rapid deterioration of printed materials, there should be national and international efforts towards their conservation and their reproduction in alternative forms. At the same time provision should be made for full bibliographic access to these materials.

5. Encouragement should be given to the conversion of printed texts to machine-readable formats and to the improved electronic transmission of such texts.

6. The conference supports the standardization of formats for the

electronic storage of humanities data. It recommends that the scholarly community should share the responsibility for selecting and storing electronic data. Such data should as far as possible be integrated into established bibliographic utilities and networks in order to ensure the fullest access.

7. The development and wide dissemination of standardized multilingual computational tools for text analysis and information retrieval should be encouraged so that these materials can be fully utilized.

8. Cost studies and evaluation techniques should be developed in order to optimize the creation and use of such tools.

9. There should be urgent and extensive discussion on the national and international copyright issues raised by technological developments, with a view to achieving a balance between the need for wide scholarly access to materials and the protection of the interests of their producers.

10. All available means should be employed to disseminate and promote these resolutions so that the combined weight of the humanities community can be committed to their implementation.

Appendix 1:
List of Contributors

Angela Blackburn   Senior Editor, Oxford University Press.

W. Robert Connor   Director of the National Humanities Center, North Carolina.

Peter Denley   Lecturer in History at Queen Mary and Westfield College, University of London.

John Forty   Principal and Vice-Chancellor of the University of Stirling.

Jean-Claude Gardin   Director of Research at the Mission Archéologique Française en Asie Centrale, Centre National de la Recherche Scientifique (CNRS), Paris.

Deian Hopkin   Senior Lecturer in History at the University College of Wales, Aberystwyth.

John Howe   Professor of American History at the University of Minnesota.

May Katzen   Director of the Office for Humanities Communication, 1982-1990.

Anthony Kenny   President of the British Academy.

George Landow   Professor of English and Art at Brown University.

Donald F McKenzie   Professor of Bibliography and Textual Criticism, University of Oxford.

Jack Meadows   Head of the Department of Library and Information Studies at Loughborough University of Technology.

J. Hillis Miller   Distinguished Professor of English and Comparative Literature at the University of California at Irvine

J. Michael Smethurst   Director General, Humanities and Social Sciences, The British Library.

Antonio Zampolli   Professor of Computational Linguistics at the University of Pisa and Director of the Institute for Computational Linguistics of the National Research Council of Italy, at Pisa.

Appendix 2:
Conference Programme

Scholarship and Technology in the Humanities
9th-12th May 1990
Elvetham Hall, Hampshire

Wednesday 9th May 1990

Afternoon   Opening Keynote Address
                                  Dr. Anthony Kenny, FBA,
                                  The President of The British Academy

                                  Discussion

Thursday 10th May 1990   *Recent Trends in Different Disciplines*

Morning   Text Based Disciplines

Literary Studies   Professor J. Hillis Miller
                                  Department of English and Comparative Literature,
                                  University of California at Irvine

Linguistics   Dr. Antonio Zampolli
                                  Director, Instituto di Linguistica Computationale,
                                  Pisa

Classical Studies   Professor W. Robert Connor
                                  Director, National Humanities Center, Research
                                  Triangle Park, North Carolina

Afternoon   Textual, Numerical and Graphics Based Disciplines

History   Dr. Peter Denley
                             Department of History, University of London
                             Dr. Deian Hopkin
                             Department of History, University College of Wales

Art History   Professor George Landow
                             Department of English and Art, Brown University

Archaeology   Professor Jean-Claude Gardin
                             Mission Archéologique Française en Asie Centrale,
                             CNRS, Paris

Friday 11th May 1990 *The Scholar and the Research Environment*

Morning   Dimensions of the Research Community

The Scholar, Technology and the Research Community
                             Professor A. Jack Meadows
                             Department of Library & Information Studies,
                             Loughborough University of Technology

The Scholar, Technology and the National Environment
                             Professor John Forty, FRSE
                             Principal & Vice-Chancellor,
                             University of Stirling

The Scholar, Technology and the International Scene
                             Dr. John Haeger
                             Vice-President for Programs and Planning,
                             The Research Libraries Group Inc.

                             Panel Discussion

Afternoon   The Scholar, Technology and Funding

The Training of the Modern Scholar
                             Professor John Howe
                             University of Minnesota

The Dissemination of Scholarly Knowledge
                             Ms. Angela Blackburn
                             Oxford University Press, Oxford

Support for Research   Panel Discussion

Saturday 12th May 1990 *Conclusions*

Morning	Concluding Synthesis
Discussion of Issues	Professor Don McKenzie, FBA Pembroke College, Oxford
Closing Address	Mr. J. Michael Smethurst Driector General, The British Library, Humanities & Social Sciences

Index